An Oasis for Mind and Spirit

Camille, Florence, and Frank (Figgi) Duane Rosengren at the store's 312 Bonham Street location, just behind the Alamo, in 1980. The store was in this location from 1959 to 1982. *Rosengren Family Collection.*

An Oasis for Mind and Spirit

*"One of the finest and most admirable
bookstores in America."*
—Willie Morris

Mary Carolyn Hollers George

Introduction by
Phil Hardberger
Mayor of San Antonio, 2005-2009

San Antonio, Texas
2015

First Edition

Hardback Edition ISBN: 978-1-60940-379-9

Special leather-bound edition ISBN: 978-1-60940-427-7

Ebook editions:
ePub ISBN: 978-1-60940-380-5
MobiPocket/Kindle ISBN: 978-1-60940-381-2
Library PDF ISBN: 978-1-60940-382-9

Wings Press
627 E. Guenther
San Antonio, Texas 78210
Phone/fax: (210) 271-7805
On-line catalogue and ordering:www.wingspress.com
All Wings Press titles are distributed to the trade by
Independent Publishers Group
www.ipgbook.com

Library of Congress Cataloging In Publication:

George, Mary Carolyn Hollers
  Rosengren's Books: An Oasis for Mind and Spirit / Mary Carolyn
Hollers George.
        pages cm.
Includes bibliographical references and index.
  ISBN 978-1-60940-379-9 (hardback : alk. paper) -- ISBN 978-1-
60940-427-7 (hardback ltd. ed. : alk. paper) -- ISBN 978-1-60940-
380-5 (epub ebook) -- ISBN 978-1-60940-381-2 (kindle-mobi-
pocket ebook) -- ISBN 978-1-60940-382-9 (library pdf ebook)
  1. Rosengren's Books--History. 2. Bookstores--Texas--San
Antonio--History--20th century. 3. Rosengren, Florence, 1905-1988.
4. Booksellers and bookselling--Texas--San Antonio--Biography. 5.
San Antonio (Tex.)--Intellectual life--20th century. I. Title.
  Z473.R72 G46 2015
  381'.4500209764351--dc23   2014032918

SFI Certified Sourcing
www.sfiprogram.org
SFI-00453
SFI label applies to text stock

For the book lovers
whose support of independent book stores
has been little short of heroic

Booksellers are generous, liberal-minded men
... anxious for the encouragement of literature.

—Samuel Johnson, 1756

A town isn't a town without a bookstore. It may
call itself a town, but unless it's got a bookstore
it knows it's not fooling a soul.

—Neil Gaiman, 2002

Independent booksellers are the bedrock of our civilization.

—Al Gore, 2013

*Thanks to Charles Butt
for a generous donation
which helped to make
this book possible.*

Contents

Introduction by Phil Hardberger   *ix*

Acknowledgments   *xv*

1. The Rosengrens: A Family of Booksellers   3
2. The Lady in the Bookstore   *11*
3. The Poe Discovery   *17*
4. San Antonio: "Skyscraping and Ancient"   *23*
5. The Florence Phenomenon   *41*
6. Parnassus Weekends in Time of War   *49*
7. Evictions and Propitious Moves   *62*
8. Common Cause   *74*
9. Small Spaces, Expansive Ideas   *82*
10. The Final Chapter   *88*
11. Onward   *99*

Appendix 1: Florence's Legacy in Texas Publishing   *103*
Appendix 2: Concerning the Rosengren Papers   *111*
Appendix 3: Frank Duane Rosengren, 1926-2010   *113*
Notes   *115*
Sources Consulted   *129*
Index   *133*

Introduction

Rosengren's Books was the remarkable mecca of intellectual thought and discussion in San Antonio for 52 years. Its owner, Florence Rosengren, along with her son, Figgi, and his wife, Camille, ran the store with professionalism and some financial success. But to describe Florence simply as a bookstore owner wildly understates the case. She was a quiet force in our community who made us think more broadly and with more wisdom than before we met her. Although the scale was smaller, she was the Madame de Stael or Sylvia Beach of South Texas. She shared in common with them the "education of the Salon," where conversations of intellectuals, artists and politicians stimulated thought, and ultimately better people. This book, written by Mary Carolyn George (no small intellectual herself), is the story of Florence and her store. It is a story worth telling and George does it well. Interestingly enough, small histories can teach more than giant tomes.

Linda and I came to San Antonio in 1970, young, newly married, with reasonably good educations, but almost no contacts, no friends and even worse for me as a lawyer, no clients. The first year or so I could have been charitably described as under-employed. As luck would have it though, this gave me enough time to explore the City, and find what bookstores were available, so I could go back to the office and read them in lieu of profitable work. At the time I thought these were hard years; now I think of them with sweet remembrances. Ah, the joys of leisure.

It wasn't long before I discovered Rosengren's Books. Upon my first visit Florence introduced herself, and began to ask me questions about my life, details about why we had decided to settle in San Antonio, what my interests were, etc. Before I knew it half of the afternoon was gone, and I was still talking about myself with an occasional nudge of "go on" from Florence. Looking back on it, I'm not sure if she was as interested as she made me feel, or simply gauging what books she would be selling me in the years ahead. Perhaps it was both. After all she was in the book selling business. But she never forgot anything I said, and never recommended anything to me that was not spot-on target. I went home that night, telling Linda I had just made a great friend. (Try duplicating that experience at Barnes and Noble someday, and see how it comes out.)

In the early months of my acquaintance, Florence was—in my eyes—a kindly grandmother who had a terrific knowledge of books, and seemingly had read everything in her store. I consistently overspent my book budget, and would often leave laden with books that I could ill afford. But apparently I wasn't the only one who overbought. Frates Seeligson, Sr., a prominent and affluent member of San Antonio nobility, once talked his wife into giving him a year's supply of books from Rosengren's as his Christmas present. It seemed like a reasonable request, and she granted it. By the time the next Christmas rolled around and she figured the toll of those books, she made it clear she wouldn't make that mistake a second time. No more free passes to Rosengren's!

But Florence did more than sell books. She was a conduit for friendships. It seemed that every time I walked into the store, she would introduce me to a few other customers who were friends of hers. She had a lot of friends, and gradually, but surely, some of her friends became my friends. She was not interested in politics as such, but she was passionately interested in thoughts, attitudes, and things. And that described many of her customers and friends. They might be Democrats, Republicans or Anarchists but that is not how they were identified in her salon. Reciting stale political slogans wouldn't get you very far with Florence. She wanted rational discourse, and if you weren't prepared to do that, better to go look for a book somewhere else in the store.

And the people: what an interesting group of characters and customers. It was the original core of our social life in San Antonio and those friendships remain until this day unless God has removed them from the scene. You walked into the store, say on a Saturday afternoon, found yourself a book, and plopped down in a comfortable well-worn chair. These chairs were everywhere, and gave you the impression of being in an aging home with an excellent library, rather than a commercial store. If you didn't have a book in mind, Florence would suggest one tailored to your interests, which she had set aside for just when you came in. Sure enough it would have a piece of yellow paper on it with your name. She really had been saving it for you. And somehow she had already read it. How she had enough time to read all these books was beyond my comprehension. But she did.

One day she came over and conspiratorially whispered that I would enjoy a book she put in my hands because it was "very sexy." I was somewhat shocked that my "grandmother" in her 60s knew what that was. But I was 30 then and now that I am older than she was then; 1 don't know why I was shocked. Some things don't go out of style. I will say that in those long ago years, "sexy" was suggestive in books rather than descriptive (with a few Henry Miller-type exceptions).

I picked my reading chairs for comfort, but also to see the passing parade of people. Here comes Maury Maverick Jr., shabbily dressed and hunched over like a washed-up boxer, grumbling about everything except the Marine Corps and purple martins, both of which he loved. Maury Jr., a writer and former State Representative, was the son of Maury Maverick Sr., the former Mayor of San Antonio. Maury Jr. growled a lot, but always with a twinkle in his eye. He once told me that he highly respected and was attracted to the non-violence of the Quaker religion. "In fact," he said, "I'm going to join the Quaker Church. I just need to kill a couple of SOBS first."

Then Herkie Bernard, an able tax lawyer, who devoted most of his nights to working with West and Southsiders, and other disadvantaged people, to get them a place at the economic table through organization. Sometimes he'd be accompanied by Ernie Cortes, a recognized genius, who became nationally famous as an organizer for justice for all people. And here comes a tall man, gray hair down to his shoulders, well-dressed, but wearing a cape and using a cane with a skull's head, for God's sake. Who would that be, you ask. Why, that was Robert L. B. Tobin, the leading collector in the United States of theater art and scene design. The Tobin Center for the Performing Arts, a magnificent building that opened in September of 2014, is named after him. The diminutive, but thoroughly scrappy man with him is John Leeper, director of the McNay Art Museum. Leeper professed to be a Democrat's democrat, but ruled the McNay with an iron hand in a most undemocratic way, while making the McNay one of the leading art museums in the country.

Charles and Margie Kilpatrick were frequently seen there. Charles was the editor and publisher of the *San Antonio Express-News*, and was loved on both sides of the border. Charles, a former Marine like Maverick, was the strong, silent type. He and Margie had a great 50-year-plus marriage, but Margie could never be described as "silent." If you were bold enough to express an opinion, you better be prepared to defend it if Margie was around. But she had to take a second seat on opinions to Mae Tuggle, the wife of a highly regarded architect, Emmit Tuggle. Mae could get a rise out of anyone, and took enjoyment in making outrageous statements. She reached an apogee along these lines when she said she was "tired of hearing about these firemen" after their heroic work and sacrifice in 9/11. Of course, everyone in the room jumped on her. She was very pleased.

Mayor Walter McAllister and other prominent politicians and businessmen would come and go. Florence moved easily around these notables, saints, sinners, scholars and eccentrics, spreading her grace, using her store as everybody's library and living room. Rosengren's Books was a salon of civilization and enlightenment that made us all better citizens.

As the shadow of our own life lengthens, we realize it is not always the great names of the day who made our lives different. Sometimes we fail to realize who is making us who we are. Sometimes it can be a little woman who runs a bookstore.

Thank you, Mary Carolyn George, for helping us to remember.

Phil Hardberger
Mayor of San Antonio, 2005-2009

Acknowledgments

Many individuals have made this book possible, but I owe a special debt of gratitude to members of the Rosengren family: Frank Duane Rosengren, Camille Sweeney Rosengren, Emily Rosengren Ferry, and, of course, to Florence.

Thanks also for the insights and information gained in the course of interviews with those whose lives were enhanced by their involvement with the Rosengrens. (See "Interviews and Correspon- dence" in Appendix 2.) Finally, many thanks to all who promptly responded to requests for information. These include, in alphabetical order, Gayla Christiansen, Brian J. Contine, Martha Doty Freeman, David Haynes, Lynn Hendry, Mary Jinks, Mike Knoop, Hannah Neal, Ann Maria Watson Pfeiffer, Morgan Exum Price, Karen Reifel, Tom Shelton, Martha Utterback, and Lyle Williams. Thanks also to Michele Stanush for an admirable index.

Special thanks also to the editor, designer and publisher of this volume, Bryce Milligan, who was privileged to work in the store, 1980-1981, and who wrote two of Florence's obituary encomiums.0

Finally, a very special thanks to Charles Butt for a generous donation which helped to make this book possible.

To you all, thank you.

Mary Carolyn Hollers George
San Antonio, Texas
2014

Rosengren's Book & Art Galleries, 609-611 North State Street in the Tree Studio Building and Annexes, Chicago, 1920s. This was Frank's first retail store, which opened in 1919. Open throughout the "Roaring 20s," the store was frequented by writers like Carl Sandburg, Max Bodenheim, Ben Hecht and Charles MacArthur, as well as the famous American bookman, Wright Howes. *Rosengren Family Collection.*

An Oasis for Mind and Spirit

. . . the best of book stores.
—Robert Frost

Knut Rosengren changed his name to Frank Rosengren before the age of 20, when a passer-by mistakenly called him "Frank" and he liked the sound. He shortened this to Frank Rose, the name he used as a "banjo-flailing baritone balladeer." His son, Frank Duane, wrote that this image, taken before 1920, was a "posed photograph for a singer in search of bookings." Known to the family as the "pretty boy picture," Frank Duane remembered that "it was nice to have a daddy who could *seem* to look like Valentino!" The photograph was taken by the C. F. Gairing Co., 128 N. LaSalle St., Chicago. *Rosengren Family Collection.*

1

The Rosengrens:
A Family of Booksellers

This is a love story—a story about the love of books—a passion that has given insight, enlightenment, and delight to untold multitudes since the invention of the printing press over five centuries ago. This is also the story of a family of booksellers, a story unlikely to be repeated and therefore worthy of retelling. The number of booksellers—described by Samuel Johnson as the "generous, liberal-minded" true patrons of literature—is shrinking daily. We mourn this loss as we move into a future where reading itself is being redefined.

The patriarch of the Rosengren family of booksellers was born in 1892 and was given the baptismal name of Knut Henning Rosengren, later to be known as Frank Rosengren. His story began when his father, a skilled carpenter whose name was later translated as "Andrew" in English, went to install a cabinet in the residence of the Archbishop of Uppsala, the Lutheran primate of Sweden.[1] There he met Cristina, a fetching young employee in the Archbishop's household. They soon married and their first two children, Carl ("Charlie") and Gerda, were born in Sweden. The family immigrated from Sweden in 1883 to the United States, where two more children, Frank and Kitty, were born. Carl would die in the flu pandemic of 1918. Andrew and Cristina made their way to the Humboldt Park area on the north side of Chicago, a community of skilled artisans—mainly northern Europeans with a preponderance of Swedish families. This may explain why Cristina would never learn to speak English. Still, she was very wise about the ways of her adopted country. Her oft-repeated advice to her son, Frank, was to "get in business for yourself."

An invaluable account of Frank Rosengren's progress in getting "in business" for himself was written in 1948—a year before his death—while he was confined in a nursing home. Titled "My Education as a Bookseller," he submitted the 20-page manuscript to Frederick Melcher, the publisher and editor of *Publisher's Weekly*. Alas, his long-time friend kindly replied in a letter dated September 20, 1948, that he could not suggest where it could be put in print. The document was subsequently lost for six decades until his son, Frank Duane Rosengren, discovered this treasure in 2008 while searching through storage boxes filled with random collections of papers. The following narrative of Frank's early life draws heavily upon this source.

From Uppsala to Chicago

When Frank finished the ninth grade, his first year of high school [ca. 1906], his father felt he could not afford to educate him and loaned him the money to finance several weeks at a business college. Frank soon had a job at $15 a week in the "commission house district" on South Water Street in Chicago. But working in the frantic Chicago financial markets was not Frank's cup of tea, and he began to think of following his real love—books. He quit his $15 a-week job and got a job as a stock boy at $7 a week at A.C. McClurg & Co.—at that time reputedly "the largest bookstore in the world." His father was apoplectic. His mother understood. He also developed a wanderlust. Each spring, he would quit his job and go hoboing about the country until the chill winds of fall drove him back to McClurg's. Apparently, he was too useful an employee to fire.

These tramp trips provided the adventure and excitement his youth craved. He worked as a lumber camp cook, a coal stoker, and a farm hand, but at other times he was more congenially employed as a singing waiter, elevator boy, or bartender. These journeys also served a higher purpose for Frank Rosengren: ". . . to see and know my country, know its people and institutions and to understand the general layout of our universities and libraries and the bookstores that served them." Second-hand and rare books were of special interest to Frank, so one year he got a job with Powner's Book Store, at that time the largest second-hand bookseller in Chicago. In less than a year, he learned all he needed to know to begin buying and selling old books and decided to become a freelance "book scout."

During the same period—the years before the first World War—when he was in his early 20s, he adopted the stage name of "Frank Rose" and attained a certain amount of success as a pop singer. One summer, he took his banjo and his big baritone voice to the Grand Hotel on Mackinac Island where he performed until the fall closing.[2] He was also featured at the Fox Lake Casino, just north of Chicago. The date there must have been 1913 or 1914; the most money he ever made before going into the book business came to him one night when he introduced a new song by the young Irving Berlin, "Take Me Back," which has a copyright date of 1913. "Big Jim" Colosimo, Chicago's crime boss prior to Al Capone, came into the club with a few bodyguards and sat down in front of the stage. "Big Jim" had just broken up with one of his numerous lady loves and was upset by the matter. He liked the song so much that he tossed Frank ten dollars and told him to sing it again. In all, Frank Rose sang "Take Me Back" thirty times in a row and made $10 each time—and $300 was an epic sum in 1913. His passion for collecting books now conjoined with his passion for collecting sheet music. He built a collection of 19th and early 20th century sheet music—more than a thousand songs—ranging from first issues of Sigmund Romberg to Stephen Foster and Irving Berlin.[3]

Near the end of World War I, his number came up and he was drafted into the military.[4] The first day when the recruits lined up, the sergeant asked, "Can anybody type?" Frank held up his hand and was put in the orderly room typing orders. This he did for two months until he also got orders for European duty. His ship departed—then turned around and returned to port. The Great War was over.

Frank's First Store

Following the declaration of Armistice in 1918, Frank Rosengren determined to open a retail bookstore of his own. With his experience as a free-lance scout—where "he learned fast because he was spending his own money"—he felt he had learned all he needed to know about buying and selling old books. And where better than Chicago? The city had already gained fame for its contributions to the development of an "American literature."

The term "Chicago Renaissance" applies to the period between 1910 and the mid-1920s, during which writers like Sherwood Anderson, Edgar Lee Masters, Carl Sandburg, Vachel Lindsey, Ben Hecht and Ring Lardner forged a style that came to be known as Chicago realism, an original national literature.[5] It was a city where books mattered.

Frank borrowed $100 and rented a first-floor apartment—actually one tremendous room with a kitchenette arrangement in the corner. In the center of the room, a table-bed contraption served as a book display counter by day and as his bed at night. With windows at eye-level to the street and signage, the space was identifiable as a place of business. Soon after he opened the shop, he stopped in at a warehouse and discovered they were preparing a fine library for sale. He offered the owner $300 for the lot, and that same day, found a bookseller friend who agreed to take the collection for $550. With this $250 quick profit, he had a little working capital.[6] Then and there, he determined to keep a ready cash reserve so that he would not have to share his best deals with other booksellers.

Frank's stock grew rapidly and in a year or so, he rented an upscale retail space at 609-611 North State Street in the Tree Studio Building.[7] With a pleasant-sized room curtained off at the rear as before, he was soon comfortably installed in his shop-cum-living quarters—but his ambitions now reached far beyond making a living. He determined to become an expert on first editions and would study incessantly to reach that goal.

After World War I, Frank observed that bibliography as well as book collecting were developing as a "science," but that considerations of

Frank Sr., in the North State Street store, mid-1920s. *Rosen-gren Family Collection.*

Frank Sr., in the "boutique" store at 500 Michigan Ave.,
ca. 1930. *Rosengren Family Collection.*

what actually constituted rarity were often carried to unreasonable extremes. He wrote: "In my examination of libraries for sale, I realized the need for a handbook that would give information regarding desirable, rare and otherwise sought-after books. As nothing of the sort had been done, I determined to write such a book myself." The book on which he would work until the end of his life would be called "The Americana," or the alternative, "A Bookhunter's Guide," and dealt mostly with first editions, but also with American music, documents and stamps.[8]

In working on the bibliography, he studied the catalogues of the better dealers the world over and observed that "studying such catalogues was the quickest way to become familiar with what the modern book collector or University librarian is most interested in." The catalogues which he now issued, mainly in the form of mimeographed bulletins, soon generated a flourishing mail-order business for Rosengren's. Among his most loyal clients was Fred Allen, the popular humorist.[9] Although Allen lived in Manhattan, when he desired a particular item, he requested that Rosengren search for a copy. Public and institutional libraries, however, were now the bookstore's main clients and required Frank to fill their needs in current books—dictionaries and fast-selling popular novels.

The success of the business posed dilemmas but a miracle was on its way. A guardian angel must have been assigned to look after the Rosengren family of booksellers well into the unforeseeable future.

2

The Lady in the Bookstore

O ne day, a young woman came into the bookstore in the Tree Studio Building. She was a student at the University of Chicago named Florence Kednay, and by all accounts was a very intelligent, elegant, auburn-haired young flapper. The near north side of Chicago was an exciting place in the 1920s, very much "the art scene," and it is remembered that Florence was always open to experience. It may be that she inherited a venturesome spirit from her mother.

Florence Kednay was born in 1905. Her father, John Vincent Kednay, was a foreman with Standard Oil of Indiana—a stable position even during the Depression years.[1] Her mother, Blanche Kednay, was a small town girl, not formally educated but a voracious reader blessed with an avid curiosity. In order to care for her younger brothers, Will and Ben, Blanche had dropped out of school in the sixth grade after the death of their mother. She never traveled farther from home than Milwaukee, but she was a "mind traveler" and her destinations were literally the ends of the earth. She collected books about polar exploration to both the North and South Pole, preferring the first-hand accounts found in journals and diaries.[2] John and Blanche Kednay also attended lectures by famed explorers Admiral Richard Byrd, Frederick Albert Cook, and others at Chicago's Field Museum. And she would have her books autographed by their authors. Explorer and artist Rockwell Kent had never heard of a woman interested in arctic exploration and he presented her with a series of engraved book plates.

The Kednays lived in a house, built ca. 1910, at 1613 Cleveland Avenue in Whiting, Indiana, an industrial town on Lake Michigan (now part of Hammond). Florence and her brothers, Jack and Joe, were educated in the Catholic schools of Whiting—a devastating experience that drove all three out of the church by the time of their graduation from high school. Their mother joined the exodus, although their father remained a staunch Catholic. Although bookish, Florence was exceedingly pretty, but she claimed that her social life was ruined by the fact that she could play the piano by ear. From the eighth grade on, she played for all the dances and was unable to join in the fun. She was "embarrassed" by this skill and yet disappointed that she would never learn to play classically.

She was also ambidextrous and a speed typist. In her senior year, she won a state-wide speed typing championship in Indianapolis. The prize—a working scholarship to the University of Chicago. As her work-study assignment, she became typist and secretary to a professor in the chemistry department, Dr. Winford Lee Lewis, who had invented Lewisite Gas, a blister gas used in World War I. She disapproved of Dr. Lewis's accomplishments but loved being at the university.

As the Fates decreed, Florence Kednay and Frank Rosengren were married. She was his third wife and 13 years his junior.[3] The match was not what her Catholic father had in mind for his lovely daughter, but when the first grandchild was born— Frank Duane—on August 8, 1926, all was well.

Florence Kednay while a student at the University of Chicago, ca. 1925. *Rosengren Family Collection.*

Blanche also accepted Frank quickly. The two were a good pair with only seven years difference in their ages. Frank was really a Pied Piper for the whole family. It was not only the charm of the man but the charm of the life of freedom and independence he represented. John Kednay, a solid working man and also a great reader, often talked about the fact that Frank was in business for himself and did not work for a boss. Frank also had the resources to locate polar exploration treasures. His birthday present for Blanche one year was a map from the Moses Pitt Atlas printed in London in 1680.

The newlyweds now made their residence in a basement apartment on Orchard Street and Florence became a valuable assistant in the bookshop. During the workday, baby Frank Duane was often cared for by his grandmother Kednay. There was also a nursemaid who—according to family legend—had once served as secretary to the famed British stage actress, Mrs. Patrick Campbell, during one of her tours of the U.S.[4] Because he was blessed with a happy disposition, the baby was nicknamed Felix by his nanny, which in baby talk he translated into "Figgi." [Felix is the Latin word for "happy" or "lucky." He would be called "Figgi" by family and friends until the day he died.] When need be, he would also spend the day at the shop with his parents. He remembered that his playpen was the store window: "When I was one-and-a-half, my blocks were books. I was the window display and would play with stacks of old books, amusing passersby."

But there were dilemmas other than child care and slow-paying library accounts, and Frank now sought Florence's opinion. As noted in "My Education As A Bookseller," Frank wrote:

> As the business grew, the store itself had grown in size. It was now a double store with two basements with more basements leased from merchants along the block—all jam-packed with tens of thousands of books. . . . What did I really want? A small bookshop with every book in stock hand-picked . . . the best store in town. . . . We decided to sell out and move to a smaller and better location. The nucleus of the new shop I would find on my own shelves, each book, as approved, would be taken out of stock and packed away.

One day while winnowing his stock, he came across a volume of miscellaneous old pamphlets, bound together and priced at twenty dollars. He had no recollection of how or why he originally acquired this item, but he did remember that three or four years earlier, it had been removed from the upstairs bookshelves and buried in the basement as unsalable.

In the years since he had acquired this oddity, Frank's knowledge of American first editions had increased tremendously. This time he recognized what he had overlooked before. One of the pamphlets turned out to be a 39-page item which included two titles by Edgar Allan Poe: *The Murders in the Rue Morgue* and *The Man That Was Used Up*. He realized that he had in his hands one of the rarest and most desirable items in all of American literature. It was a classic example of "the romance of book collecting."

Rosengren's Books at 500 Michigan Ave., Chicago, 1930. This store was next door to the Wrigley Building and directly across from the Chicago Tribune Tower, where the Michigan Ave. Bridge began (see the bridge railings to the left). The date visible on the gable indicates that the structure was built in 1880. *Rosengren Family Collection.*

3

The Poe Discovery

Questions in need of authoritative answers were raised by the Poe before it could be resold. The gathering of pamphlets in which it was included had been bound together in a "half-calf" leather binding and titled simply "Miscellany"—a curious collection of orations, prison reports and the like. Some covers had been removed—such was the case with the Poe—and since the cover was also the title page, it would be difficult to identify it as the genuine first edition. Only three other copies were then known to exist and one of these was in the Morgan Library in New York. Frank determined to compare his pamphlet with the Morgan copy. But first things first. The State Street shop was selling out and the sale must go on. It took six months but the closeout was a tremendous success. The public flocked into the shop and toward the end, job lots went to other booksellers, followed by a final auction. Rosengren Booksellers now moved to 500 North Michigan Avenue next door to the Wrigley Building and directly across from the Chicago Tribune Tower. The ramshackle old building, built in 1880, was due for demolition and the roof leaked, but there was a sidewalk-level window and the rent was two hundred dollars a month. And it was a great location.

After getting settled in the new shop, Frank took his Poe to New York where comparison with the Morgan Library copy proved beyond doubt that it was a genuine first edition, published by

Poe himself in 1843. While there, Frank called on several dealers who had no interest in even looking at the book. But before going forward, he telephoned Harry Hansen, whose syndicated column "The First Reader" appeared in many newspapers. A full column was devoted to the Poe story.

On September 28, 1929, J. K. Lilly—a major collector of the works of Poe—received a letter from a book dealer in Evanston, Illinois, who gave the details of the Rosengren discovery and posed the question: "How would you like to own a First Edition of *Murders in the Rue Morgue*?"[1] Lilly purchased the Poe for $13,000. The sale was made just a few days before the stock market crash of October 29, 1929, and Frank still had the cash in his pocket. The Evanston dealer received $500 for his help. Frank also paid a long-standing debt to his father:

> After relating the tale of how I had sold a book for such an agreeable amount, my father quietly said, "After all, I guess you knew best." I knew he was thinking of the day when I came home with my joyous news of quitting a job that paid $15 a week for one that paid $7. I also knew that I had made more profit on this transaction than he had been able to earn in his first years in the United States.

With the publicity his discovery received, the editor of the "Mid-Week Magazine" section of the *Chicago Daily News* suggested that Frank do an article on modern first editions.

He was keen to share this information, convinced that there were rare and sought-after

Frank Duane, Florence, and Frank Sr. in the North State Street store, late 1920s. *Rosengren Family Collection.*

books scattered in all sorts of odd places throughout the land—and whose owners had no idea of their value. The first article was titled "There's Gold on the Top Shelf."

The response was so positive that the newspaper asked him to do a talk on the subject over their radio station. Shortly after that, another article appeared titled "More Gold on the Bottom Shelf."

Meanwhile, the new shop was doing none too well. The Depression was on and gangsters ruled Chicago. The shop was broken into and robbed three times in as many months. When the year's lease was up in 1930, the store again went out of business. But this allowed Frank and Florence to go on a belated honeymoon to Europe—six weeks in England, Germany, and France—discovering old world culture together. Figgi stayed with his Kednay grandparents and the story of his parents' travels came to him in chapters.

Shortly after their return, the Rosengrens moved to Evanston, Illinois, and Frank worked full time on his Americana bibliography. Alas, after two years, he realized that he had tackled a job that was endless. And the need to earn a living was pressing. The year was 1933. Franklin Delano Roosevelt had just been elected president and it seemed the country would survive. They were living in a brick duplex on Noyes Avenue at the time and their neighbors, the Brandos, urged them to give the book business another chance. Marlon Brando Sr. and his wife, Dorothy ("Dodie"), pitched in with hammer and paint brushes to prepare a new shop for opening. Eight-year-old Frank Duane was supposed to play with the Brando son, Marlon, who was two years older and proved to be bigger and tougher, and always wanted to wrestle. The Rosengrens now opened a new store at 1741 Sherman Avenue in Evanston, not far from the Northwestern University campus—a few weeks before FDR closed the banks.

But soon, a more immediate problem developed. Doctors diagnosed Frank Duane with a severe bronchial ailment and said that his chances of surviving another northern winter were dubious. Grandmother Kednay and her grandson would spend the winter of 1934-35 in Tucson, Arizona. The prospect of being separated from their son each winter was too bleak. Frank described the three Rosengrens' journey as they "headed south in our brand new Ford to find a new home where the climate was right and the chosen city seemed to hold business possibilities. We considered Dallas and Santa Fe—but drove on. We came to a ridge overlooking the city of San Antonio, Texas. The panorama that spread before us was extremely beautiful, clean and green. I murmured to myself, 'This is it,' and this proved to be true." They returned to Evanston to pack and ship book stock and household possessions and were back in San Antonio to stay by late summer of 1935.

Actually, Harry Hertzberg, a prominent San Antonio lawyer, civic leader, state senator, and prolific collector of rare books—often from Rosengren's various locations—had long campaigned to persuade the Rosengrens to relocate to San Antonio.[2] He felt that Frank's expertise and extroverted character would guarantee success and argued "you are just another bookstore in Chicago which is loaded with bookstores." In a letter dated January 5, 1929, Hertzberg had written to Frank asking him to visit, and optimistic of a positive outcome: "When you arrive, you will know [San Antonio] by the fact that the people are more courteous, the highways better, the climate more salubrious, the odor of the stockyards missing, and you will find that people are thinking of something else besides how to skin each other. I am not surprised that you do not know that there are no Indians here." Humorous banter often flavored exchanges between Frank and his friends.

While the diagnosis of Frank Duane's respiratory condition was several years in the future at the time of the Hertzberg letter, mention of the healthful climate would weigh heavily in their decision. Long favored as a health resort, the Chamber of Commerce motto at the time was "San Antonio: where the sunshine spends the winter."

4

San Antonio:

"Skyscraping and Ancient"

In Harry Hertzberg's 1929 letter encouraging Frank Rosengren to move his family to San Antonio, he jested about the ignorance of those from the Northeast and the Midwest about his beloved hometown. But San Antonio's reputation as a charming, healthy, almost Edenic spot had been celebrated for nearly a century by numerous writers, including Sydney Lanier, who somehow found time to write a history of the city and play flute with the local Männerchor during his short visit, and O. Henry, who set several short stories in the city. Other literary visitors attracted to the city had run the gamut from Oscar Wilde to Stephen Crane to William Butler Yeats, not to mention "Teddy" Roosevelt.

A few years later—in February 1938—the globe-trotting English novelist Graham Greene spent a few days in San Antonio's new Plaza Hotel en route to Mexico by train and grasped the city's magic. On a postcard to his wife, he wrote: "Very hot, palmy, old Spanish cathedral, a river winding in and out of town, very clean and skyscraping and ancient at the same time." About the cathedral—San Fernando, which dates from 1758—he wrote "Mass in Spanish, the old archbishop very sweet and useless."[1] Although Greene never returned to Texas, San Antonio was one of only two American cities that he liked, the other being San Francisco. "Skyscraping and ancient" defines the choices that the Rosengrens made upon their arrival—skyscraping, the Milam Building where their bookstore would be located for the first decade, and ancient, the Zambrano house where they would make their home forever more.

Although he overestimated the number of rare book collectors in South Texas who could support the store in the middle of the Great Depression, the Rosengrens had an enlightened advisor in Harry Hertzberg. He had certainly prepared the ground for their arrival, resulting in a fine showing of Southern hospitality. Writing seven years later, George Sessions Perry described this in his *Texas: A World in Itself:*

> . . . Frank Rosengren and his wife hit San Antonio with . . . a sick boy and the intention of opening a book shop. The probability that the book shop would succeed was extremely slight. Yet for some mysterious reason, Frank felt immediately that he'd come not to a strange land, but home.
>
> A week or so later on Christmas morning, when Frank went outside his door, he almost broke his neck he stumbled over so many Christmas presents. And for the rest of the day these theoretically lonely strangers hadn't a second to call their own—so many people were calling up to see if they wouldn't come over for a drink of whiskey and a piece of fruit cake.
>
> Now it doesn't take any special powers of discernment to know that the Rosengrens are of the good people of this earth. But it does, I think, if you haven't even seen them. Anyway, that's what happened. In the few years this Yankee family has lived in the somewhat rough and rusty and genuine old city of San

Antonio, it's collected more real friends than it ever had anywhere else.[2]

Harry Hertzberg was perfectly in tune with the sensibilities of the Rosengrens in both domestic and business matters. The first and most important question—a school for their precocious son, Frank Duane (hereafter referred to as "Figgi"). The River Road Country Day School, founded in 1926 by Hetty Browne, was ranked among the top ten progressive schools in the U.S. during its decade of existence.[3] A country school in the city—it was located at 445 River Road on a five-acre tract that was bounded by Anastacia on the north and East Magnolia on the south. The River Road neighborhood is an enclave nestled along the southern edge of Brackenridge Park—370 acres of woodlands and trails under great oaks. Through it meanders the San Antonio River, which rises in a cluster of springs near the "Blue Hole" headwaters spring, just above the northern boundary of the park. The neighborhood is favored typically—then and now—by artists and architects, writers, musicians, and intellectuals.

There was only one significant building on the property when it was acquired—the Zambrano Homestead, occupied since 1780. Located on land granted to the Zambrano family by the King of Spain in 1776, the house was built by Macario Zambrano, a prominent rancher whose sons were important political figures in the early nineteenth century.[4] The house was "rammed earth" construction with foot-thick exterior walls. The property received a Texas Historic marker in 1966.

The Zambrano house was used as an art studio for Country Day School students until soon after

The River Road Country Day School, 445 River Road in San Antonio, Texas, ca. 1929. The building was constructed of concrete blocks, plastered to resemble adobe. *Frank Duane Rosengren collection, Daughters of the Republic of Texas Library at the Alamo.*

Frank Duane ("Figgi") attended the River Road Country Day School for two years. The experimental school, founded in 1926 by Hetty Browne, was located on five acres beside the San Antonio River at 445 River Road. Here the students enjoy a window theater performance in the Zambrano House, which served as a studio for the school, and in 1936 became the Rosengrens' permanent home. *Frank Duane Rosengren collection, Daughters of the Republic of Texas Library at the Alamo.*

Figgi's matriculation. When the school finally began to founder, the Rosengrens rented, then purchased the house at the end of 1936 for $600.

An ancient acequia route runs alongside the property—the *Acequia labor de arriba* (the "upper labor" irrigation ditch)—which was begun in 1776 and diverted water for irrigation from the San Antonio River headwaters.[5] At some point in the 1920s, a cottage located toward the rear of the grounds of the Alamo was purchased by the Brownes and moved—via horse-drawn wagon—to the school property where it was re-constructed. It too was used as a studio and referred to as "the Jacalita" (now 114 Anastacia).

The concept of a Spanish farmhouse inspired the building that would be the central feature of the school compound. The construction was of pre-cast concrete block—a material popular at the time, trademarked Nelstone—fireproof and also the best substitute for adobe.[6] Wood elements were of hand-hewn cypress (harvested in Sisterdale, Texas), oiled and left in its natural state. Architectural details such as beamed ceilings, characteristic of adobe dwellings, provided an appropriate setting for collections of primitive Mexican art.

The faculty was as unconventional as the campus. They brought credentials from institutions that did not revere traditional teaching methods. All were women of considerable scholarly, artistic, literary and intellectual abilities; they were among the first generation of women to receive university educations—as was Florence Rosengren herself. Miss Hetty Browne, founder and director of the River Road Country Day School, received her bachelor's and master's degrees from Teacher's

College, Columbia University, where she was much influenced by the philosophy of Professor John Dewey, an educational reformer whose ideas about progressive education matched her own. Sibyl Browne, her daughter and co-director of the school (1926-1930), was similarly educated and returned to teach art education at Columbia in 1930. Rowena Green [later Fenstermaker], the school's business manager, was a graduate of Antioch College in Ohio, where the educational approach blended practical work experience with classroom instruction and participatory community governance. Mary Vance Green, an artist and Rowena's sister, also graduated with an advanced degree from Columbia University. She would later be in charge of craft design for the National Youth Administration's role in the restoration of historic La Villita in the late 1930s. Both Sibyl and Mary also studied with Diego Rivera in Mexico. Inéz Sawyer had studied at the Froebel League in New York City as well as studying natural dance with Martha Graham.[7]

According to the school's 1929 catalog, the faculty attempted to stimulate its student body of two- to twelve-year-olds "to useful or aesthetic creating, the joyous doing of things their lives demand" by combining discipline with uninhibited teaching methods. A generation who would become the makers of San Antonio, indeed the makers of South Texas, are listed in the roster of students that year: Carrington, Nixon, Houston, Armstrong, James, Giesecke, Maverick, and Dickson to name but a few. Alas, too few examples survive of these creative approaches to learning. Inéz Sawyer had the boys play football in "slow-motion" to imaginary music. Figgi remembered that the teachers let the fourth grade classes listen to the World Series on the radio as a way of incorporating math and statistical skills. Many of the students found inspiration for the directions their lives would follow. One instance of such a path: When he was ten, Figgi wrote plays that the students would perform. That same year, his play, "The Nuts at the Roundtable," was published in *Story Parade* magazine. Using the pen name Frank Duane, he later had significant success as author, playwright, screenwriter, and producer.[8]

Multiple factors forced the closure of the River Road Country Day School in 1937, eleven years after its founding, foremost among them the deepening Depression and the war clouds that were gathering the world over. Whether or not it was a Utopia, striving for perfection and doomed to fail, it was a life-enhancing experience for the children privileged to attend the school. For sixth and seventh grades, Figgi attended St. Martin's Hall, an experimental school operated by Our Lady of the Lake University—commuting by bus—then graduated from Thomas Jefferson High School in 1944.

The amenities of living in the River Road neighborhood, almost surrounded by Brackenridge Park and its golf course, were fully exploited by the Rosengren family. In that period, most of these were free—swimming in the river at Lambert's Beach, the Witte Museum, the golf course, and the world-class zoological garden. The Brackenridge Stable with miles of bridle paths through the park was nearby—especially convenient because with the purchase of the Zambrano house came a stable with two horses. One named "Chiquita" was a favorite.

River Road was an old neighborhood, even by San Antonio standards, having evolved over the

Florence Rosengren, a neighbor, Figgi, and a goat (one of their many "pets-with-personalities"). *Rosengren Family Collection.*

past century and a half around the Zambrano homestead, and it had become something of a multi-ethnic island. The Rosengrens' close neighbors included three Anglo families, three African-American families and four Hispanic families.[9]

Our Lady of Sorrows Catholic Church, 3107 North St. Mary's Street, was built in 1915, and the parish included both the River Road neighborhood and the area known at the time as "La Piedrera," after the old rock quarry that was developed in the 1920s as the Sunken Garden Theater and the Japanese Tea Garden.[10] With Florence Rosengren's interest in music, she was surely present when Max Reiter, a young German conductor and refugee from anti-Semitism in Europe, organized a trial orchestra concert in June of 1939 at the Sunken Garden

Theater. Moved by the success of this concert, the Symphony Society of San Antonio was formally incorporated.

To return to Graham Greene's observation that San Antonio was "skyscraping and ancient at the same time"—it was surely the contrast that appealed to him. At that time, skyscrapers were not considered appropriate in his ancient London where Foyles Bookshop, at five stories, was among the tallest buildings in town.[11] It was Harry Hertzberg's plan that Frank's new shop be located in the Milam Building, at first on the sixth floor because nothing else was available. But by the winter of 1936, the Frank Rosengren Book Shop was located at street level two doors east of the entrance to the building which was on the northeast corner of Travis Street and Soledad.

The Milam Building, built in 1928, was designed by George Willis who, early in his career, ca. 1900, had served as a draftsman in the Oak Park, Illinois, office of Frank Lloyd Wright. At the time of its construction, it was the nation's tallest brick and reinforced-concrete structure and also the first high-rise, air-conditioned office building in the country.[12] Two other skyscrapers were built at the same time in downtown San Antonio: the Plaza Hotel (1927), 311 South St. Mary's Street, and the distinctive Smith-Young Tower (1929), 310 South St. Mary's, both designed by the firm of Atlee B. and Robert M. Ayres. [The names of both buildings have changed through the years.] Full-page ads for the Milam Building in the *San Antonio City Directory* for 1935-1940 devote an entire paragraph to the air-conditioning system that "circulates fresh air so that every office has a complete change of air every seven

The Milam Building at the northeast corner of Travis Street and Soledad Street in San Antonio, built in 1928, seen from the Southeast. The Frank Rosengren Book Shop was located first on the sixth floor, then at street level, two doors east of the main entrance on Travis Street. *Zintgraff Studio Photograph Collection, MS 355, Z-2126-M-7. University of Texas at San Antonio Libraries Special Collections from the Institute of Texan Cultures.*

minutes . . . which increases efficiency and eliminates the irritating electric fan."

The building housed a "who's who" of old-guard Texas gentlemen of business. They had diverse occupations but almost all shared an interest in reading and "serious books."[13] The 1940-41 city directory listed ten investment houses among the tenants, including Dewar, Robertson & Pancoast and Merrill Lynch Rauscher Pierce. There were also: 139 oil industry-related businesses, including Gilcrease Oil Co., Slick-Urschel Oil Co., and Preston Northrup, the oil and gas division of the Texas Railroad Commission; 36 insurance firms; and 40 attorneys. Among the attorneys was Walter Loughridge who, after Harry Hertzberg's death in 1940, became the Rosengrens' business and legal advisor. The second floor was occupied by Guaranty Abstract Title Company, owned by Emmett Sweeney, a future in-law of Frank and Florence. There there was also an excellent cafeteria, long gone, and a quite elegant oak and walnut-paneled post office, unused now, but still there.

In the final paragraph of "My Education as a Bookseller," Frank Rosengren describes the fateful role reversals within the family business:

> We weren't long in our new shop before my wife took over the buying of new and current books and became more or less general manager of the shop. My job was to build a Rare Book Department and prepare its catalogues. . . . Among the new books [were] current best sellers, of course, and then the best editions of the best books publishers keep in print.

During much of this time, from 1936 through the early 1940s, Frank also was the Texas representative for Random House. Bennett Cerf, one of the founders of the publishing house—known for his compilations of jokes and puns, as was Frank—was a great friend from Chicago days and would spend time at the store and also as a house guest at 104 Anastacia. After 1950, Cerf became a familiar figure as a panelist on the popular television game show, "What's My Line."

Concerning the role of the publisher's rep as well as its decline, Frank Duane wrote: "No discussion of a bookstore outside New York, much less as far away as San Antonio, can be complete without the input of publisher's reps, who were far more than salesmen. . . . They provided a liaison between publishers and bookstores but were also an information conduit the other way around. It was through reps that bookstores talked to publishers."[14]

Frank Sr. also now sought escape from the heat of Texas summers that had been so beneficial to his son's health. With the onset of symptoms of the rheumatoid arthritis that had crippled his sister, Kitty, he was convinced that the San Antonio summers were making him sick, believing the climate to be "totally unnatural for a Viking."[15] In 1938, he took his first solo trip to Europe—to Sweden, "looking for his roots." He traveled by Swedish freighter from the Port of Galveston as he would the following summer of 1939 en route to London. But Europe was not his only escape from the Texas heat. Frank spent the summers of 1940 and 1941 in cool, high—and very economical—Mexico City. After that, he became too ill to travel.

In concluding "My Education as a Bookseller," Frank focused on his passion—building a rare book department—and he enumerated a few of his treasures: "The Rare Book Department has fine bindings, but also one might encounter such books as Dr. Johnson's *Dictionary*, London, 1755; the King James Bible, London, 1611; or Cardinal Newman's *Apologia Pro Vita Sua*, London, 1864, in its eight original parts, all in their correct issues of the first editions."[16] Decades later, customers could clearly recall other rarities they saw in the store, such as: a 1582 Rheims New Testament; a signed Handel symphony; numerous first editions of works by Richardson, Fielding, Shelley, Keats, and Byron; and a complete set of sheet music by Stephen C. Foster.

Frank had earlier stated that "he studied the catalogues of the better dealers in rare books throughout the world." There were few booksellers more distinguished than Maggs Bros. Ltd., located from 1938 to the present at 50 Berkeley Square, Mayfair, London. In the summer of 1939, with World War II imminent, Maggs Bros. was reducing inventories and prices were low. The treasures Frank enumerated were purchased mainly at Maggs. He arrived in London with orders to fill for his San Antonio clients—"the Herffs, Daisy Heard, Gilcrease, Hertzberg and everybody else." And he purchased a tremendous number of books for the shop. Frank would have dealt with Frank Maggs who was in charge of the travel department, "hence Americans."[17] After the war, when the then mayor of San Antonio, Maury Maverick Sr., visited Maggs Bros. at the suggestion of the Rosengrens, he made Frank Maggs an Honorary Admiral in the Texas Navy.[18]

Before Frank's return trip to the U.S., the war in Europe broke out. That he, along with massive wooden crates of books, was aboard a Swedish freighter—not yet vulnerable to Nazi attacks—was fortunate. When the shipment reached San Antonio, the job of ripping the crates apart fell to Figgi, who transformed the debris into a club house.

In addition to the clients for whom Frank filled orders at Maggs, the tenants of the Milam Building were a "rather civilized bunch of people." In short, there was no better place that a bookstore could have been located. There was no need to advertise. "The local people knew who and where we were. The out-of-towners found us." For example, Hal Dewar, senior partner of an investment house on the eleventh floor, would come down to the bookstore after his office closed. Florence might be keen to go home but she would stay as long as he wanted to sit and read.[19]

Farther afield, members of the King Ranch family were often in the shop. Texas historian and bibliophile Al Lowman observed:

> Rosengren's was the northern anchor of the old cattle country and served the whole area. The big Texas ranching families were often of Scottish, English or Irish descent with a high regard for education. Their sons were sent east to school—married college-educated eastern girls—who found the "uncultured" South Texans boring. Then they found Rosengren's and began to establish fine personal libraries. Florence was nothing less than a mother figure and offered maternal support.[20]

There were also book collectors in many South Texas towns—the store's list of customers with charge accounts included several in ranching towns as small as Refugio.

And then there was the Mexico trade. Many visitors from Mexico did *all* their Christmas book shopping at Rosengren's, while residing at the nearby St. Anthony Hotel. Of note, the Mexican Consulate office was on the second floor of the Milam Building, but word of the excellent book store in San Antonio was also spread by Texans with ranching interests in Mexico. Bobby Barclay was in Rosengren's daily when he was not at La Babia, his ranch in Musquiz, Coahuila (originally the site of a Spanish presidio garrisoned in 1774). Bobby owned the upper ranch. His cousin, Hal Goggan, another customer, owned the lower ranch. Together the ranches once comprised almost 450,000 acres.

Opportunities to meet literary greats who were at the store for book signings or simply for a visit were among the myriad factors that drew readers to Rosengren's.[21] The fact was, writers liked the Rosengrens, they liked the store, and they liked San Antonio, a combination that turned a simple bookstore into a true cultural center with an international reputation. Early authors who visited included Edith and Osbert Sitwell, Katherine Anne Porter, J. Frank Dobie, Theodor Seuss Geisel—"Dr. Seuss"—and Robert Frost. Publishers Alfred Knopf and Bennett Cerf were habitual visitors.

Robert Frost liked the place so well that he and his wife, Eleanor, chose to spend the winter of December 1936-March 1937 in San Antonio—ostensibly for health reasons. They took up residence at 113 E. Norwood Court, about one mile northwest of River Road. The Rosengrens hosted the poet's sixty-third birthday at the store in March.

Above: The iconographic photograph of Robert Frost, inscribed in white ink, "Wishing to be remembered in the best of bookstores." *Rosengren Family Collection.*

Below: Frost at Rosengren's on March 23, 1937, during a birthday celebration for him held by Frank Sr. and Florence. Frost departed San Antonio on his actual birthday, March 26. *San Antonio Light Photograph Collection, MS 359, L-1544-P. UTSA Libraries Special Collections from the Institute of Texan Cultures.*

Frost also like to "hold court and pontificate" at the store, and is remembered as being "very conscious of himself," as well he might. The four-time winner of the Pulitzer Prize was the most popular of poets—perhaps the most popular American writer of the time—and a sought-after speaker who was described as "one of the great teachers and talkers of his age." His framed photograph, inscribed "Wishing to be remembered in the best of bookstores. –Robert Frost," would be proudly displayed in the store until the day it closed.[22]

Frank Duane Rosengren's observations follow:

> The store's position as the literary center of San Antonio was, in a sense, a collaborative effort and a lucky accident. Writers from all over the world, some of them famous, came to it because they'd heard it was the place to be; serious readers from Texas and Mexico came to meet the writers; the stock grew more and more varied, and even exotic, because of the taste and demands of those who shopped there. For small-town Florence, the store afforded a constant learning experience and she was smart as hell and learned fast.

.

5

The Florence Phenomenon

Although Florence had left Catholicism as a teenager, she continued to have kindly notions about nuns, and would eventually donate her collection of signed first editions to the library of Incarnate Word College, now the University of the Incarnate Word. She had a clear picture of the female who dedicates herself to service, and she admired that role. An interesting aspect of her sense of her own "mission" is that she defined her service to the community as part of a commercial enterprise—except she did not run the bookstore like a commercial enterprise. It was love—it was her life. She was as dedicated to it as if she had gone into a nunnery.[1]

Until Frank could not physically write, he kept his hand in, ordering rare books and publishing catalogues. He also handled the billing—which usually included poems that were reassuring evidence that his delicious sense of humor survived his infirmity. But the bookstore was now managed by Florence, and her strongly-held beliefs surfaced.

In his "My Education as a Bookseller," Frank wrote how Florence had stocked the new store—"of course, the best sellers." His shops in Chicago had dealt with classic rare erotica as well as banned books like the controversial *Lady Chatterley's Lover* (1928) by D.H. Lawrence. Florence, however, would have no truck with the salacious.[2] If a customer asked for something that was particularly tawdry or "not smart," her reply would be, "Oh no, we do not have that kind of thing." She would look askance and roll her eyes a little bit. She would willingly engage in intellectual debate about someone's particular interest in an author, but her Catholic upbringing would prevail—most of the time. But a new work of literature by a major modern writer such as Henry Miller was unaccountably acceptable—although his first published books, *Tropic of Cancer* (1934) and others, were banned in the United States "on grounds of obscenity." [After Frank's death in 1949, some of his erotica collection went into a series of bonfires, though some of the rarest items were purchased by two of the bookstores' best customers.]

Florence's energy was prodigious. She was an excellent cook and especially enjoyed baking bread. Authors in town for a book signing, publishers' representatives, and regular customers became friends and were invited to dinner at the magical house on Anastacia which had been restored and gradually enlarged. John Dos Passos—at the height of literary success for his *U.S.A.* trilogy of novels and considered one of the finest novelists of his time—is remembered "sitting on the couch eating strawberries and cream and freshly-baked bread and butter and having a wonderful time."[3] Also among their early guests were architect Henry Steinbomer and his wife, Dorothy, a well-known artist, along with their young daughter, Shirley. Frank was then a sturdy man with great bushy eyebrows and he was delighted when Shirley observed that "you look just like the wind."[4]

Early on, for a short time, Florence and a group of friends formed a poetry reading group which met at the shop on Thursday evenings—when all the stores downtown were open: Dorothy Steinbomer, author Janette Sebring Lowrey, and Frank Drought, the son of Mrs. Henry P. Drought, were among the regulars. Mrs. Drought's Sunday evening salons at 1215 North St. Mary's Street (now on the campus of Providence High School and not far from River Road) was another place where many of San Antonio's most creative people came together—including the Rosengrens. Once a guest, always welcome. Mrs. Drought was a person who made things happen, accepting as her personal mission the enhancement of the cultural assets of the city [President of the San Antonio Art league, 1913-1938, charter member of the San Antonio Conservation Society in 1924 and a member of the Board of Trustees of the San Antonio Public Library]. Musicians in town for a concert appearance came as honored guests but were often inspired to give impromptu performances.[5]

THE BOOKSTORE AND THE LIBRARIES

Old-line South Texans quickly accepted the Rosengren family—a rare occurrence. But the viability of the bookstore in the Milam Building during that first decade actually depended on a symbiotic relationship between Florence and the staff members of public and institutional libraries, as well as those on the several military bases in the area, working together to serve a far broader constituency. The San Antonio Public Library was housed in a new building on Market Street, begun before the Crash of 1929, but their budget had been slashed by the city. To quote an annual report's summary of 1930-1940: "As unfortunate as it was to be deprived of good books at a time when they were sadly needed, these trying years led many to their Public

Library for the help, solace and inspiration that only good books can give. Thus it was that the use of San Antonio's Public Library grew to serve a greater, more far-reaching need in the community."[6]

In 1936, in response to "the plea of thousands who found books an essential aid in their daily living," support for the library was significantly increased. But there was a problem and Harry Hertzberg—mastermind of the Rosengrens' move from Chicago and long a member of the library's Board of Trustees—had the answer.[7] It was surely he who introduced Florence to the library staff: Julia Ellen Grothaus, director from 1933-1957; Irene Francis, her assistant; Leah C. Johnston, children's department; and Juanima Wells, librarian for the Bexar County Free Library, an early "Bookmobile" program which delivered books for young and old to remote rural sections of the county.

In Frank Duane Rosengren's unpublished essay, "The Bookstore and the Libraries," written to supplement research for this book, he wrote:

> The Library Ladies were delighted. They'd been trying to deal directly with New York publishers, who barreled right over them for years. And here, all of a sudden, was a University Lady just like them and who knew how to "talk publisher." Traditionally, all Florence's ordering had been done directly from the publishers. Her big advantage was that she maintained active, open accounts with more than half-a-hundred of these, all who knew her and none of which had any interest in dealing with individual orders, even from institutions. . . . The basic structure of the deal was simple. The Librarians would draw up a

list of books they needed to order, give it to Florence, who would then place the order. As it worked out, since she was getting advance catalogues and meeting two or three dozen publishers' reps two to four times a year, she became instrumental in advising her friends, the Librarians, on what they needed.

It was a two-way street, and Florence learned from the very knowledgeable library staff.

Not only did the store make money on the deal—most publishers gave booksellers 40 percent discounts—the library saved money as the store gave the library 20 percent. It also allowed the new store to make a greater impression on publishers' sales departments because Rosengren's ordered more books than the average independent store or department store book department could.[8]

And the library also got something: "The store did the actual ordering, using its established credit accounts to pay. It received shipments, unpacked them, checked for condition and returned damaged books, repacked the books and called the library to send a truck."

In the years following World War II, the discount structure established for new books had to be adjusted for foreign items, primarily from England and France, due to exchange rates, import duties, and the like. British publications were a major item at the store because they had not been previously available in San Antonio. In fact, the Oxford University Press was one of the store's top suppliers.

Soon, there was another complicated customer— the numerous military base libraries. It was Army and Air Force policy to buy locally when possible and to follow the lead of local governmental entities when doing so. Fort Sam Houston, Kelly Field, Brooks Field, Randolph Field, Lackland Training Base—after a while, Florence was doing the ordering for an array of military institutions and that would go on long after the war years. Dale Ogden, the librarian at Kelly Field, was a "workaholic" who really knew books and ran an exemplary operation. He was delighted to find that Florence was more than competent to fill orders promptly.

In the 1950s, public libraries began to be required by municipal governments to put book purchases out for competitive bidding—to jobbers or other distributors.[9] But when one door closes, another opens. A new campus for Trinity University was under construction on Stadium Drive, over-looking the skyline of San Antonio. The George Storch Memorial Library was among the first twelve buildings to be completed in 1955. John Abbott, in charge of book acquisitions for the new library, would come into Rosengren's with requests from faculty, staff, and even President James W. Laurie (1952-1970). He would start pulling books from the shelves, transport his selections back to Trinity, then compile a list and submit it for accounting purposes. Without the libraries—public, institutional, and military—the bookstore would have survived, but this relationship granted Florence the privilege of eschewing many usual commercial considerations. It was often observed that at meetings of the American Booksellers Association and assorted book fairs, Florence Rosengren was the first bookseller whom the publishers sought out.[10]

Florence depended upon Sue Shields to manage the children's book "department"—to know what was "new, good, and important;" to make sure the shelves were always stocked with both classics and the best new work; and to have seasonal titles on hand in time to be seasonal. Sue was also the store's storyteller, and is fondly remembered as such to this day. But if Sue was the "story lady" to children, Florence was the "book lady."

Emily Rosengren Ferry remembers that people frequently said to her things like: "Your grandmother taught me to read. Your grandmother gave me my interest in books. She was always so patient with me. I am now an archeologist because she gave me a book about archeology when I was eight. Her interest in children and children's literature . . . the special children's section with little tables and chairs. [She was] always looking for the best children's books and turning me and every other young person she knew on to them."[11]

And Florence Rosengren gave of herself in other ways as well, as described in a letter written by bookseller John Douglas:[12]

> The first time I saw the Rosengrens and their bookstore, I was four years old. My two-year-old brother and six-year-old sister were usually taken care of by others and when Mother wanted to go to Rosengren's (which she often did) she had to take me with her. The bookstore was my baby-sitter. I remember my first visit. Mrs. Rosengren took me by the

hand, led me to the children's area, told me that the little chair was my chair and that I should sit in it and read a book. On the many visits, I remember friendly faces, kind words and, forever, waiting for Mother to finish talking to Mrs. Rosengren at the counter. I never knew what they were talking about or why. I do remember that on the way home, Mother was happier and more relaxed. My father worked mostly out of town so our family was three children and Mother most of the time. I believe our trips to Rosengren's were not so much to purchase the latest books but to enjoy adult conversation with intelligent, caring and listening grown-ups. . . . I am very grateful for the Rosengrens, their bookstore and their blessing to my Mother and helping her to keep her sanity. I am also grateful for the influences that caused me to love books and their importance to our world and society— and leading me to have two independent bookstores myself. Every city should have a place like Rosengren's, a place where little children discover books, where lonely people can be with others, make friends, have adult conversations and yes—even keep our sanity.

Again, Emily Rosengren Ferry: "She had that great love that kept the energy going—a life dedicated to books. . . . Again, the Catholic girl—but unlike a nun's study of God—the study of literature was her life."[13]

6

Parnassus Weekends
in Time of War

Since the founding of the city, Spanish, Mexican, Texan, and finally U.S. troops had been garrisoned downtown or nearby. By 1880, the building of Fort Sam Houston was in full swing and it was soon recognized as a well-planned and aesthetically inspiring environment. World War I saw the birth of military aviation at Fort Sam and Kelly Field. Still, it was not until the U.S. declared war upon the Axis powers in early December, 1941, that the military presence in the city escalated dramatically. But as Figgi Rosengren remembered:

> It was a very sleepy town, a cultural wasteland. Bars were really bars, restaurants were really hash houses unless they were private (and expensive) clubs. Draftees with cultural and intellectual interests (or even just pretensions) had a great deal of trouble finding each other in the brief frame of a weekend pass. The Bookstore served as a magnet for the best and brightest of these. . . . Saturday mornings, sometimes starting Friday evenings, there would be a convergence. Though they did not buy many books, they were actively discovering each other . . . they knew so much . . . and talked so intensely about all sorts of sophisticated East Coast things.[1]

Frank's health deteriorated throughout the war years, and eventually Florence carried the whole load—valiantly running the shop, doing the bookkeeping—everything to keep the overhead as low as possible. The shop had one part-time salesperson, future playwright and novelist Josefina Niggli, and Verdayne Jernigan, the stock clerk. Florence valued Verdayne as "the best stock clerk she had ever had," partly because she was less of a reader than others and did not waste time browsing. Josefina was typical of the so-called sales personnel who worked with Florence in the shop. Born in Monterrey, she was sent out of Mexico as a child to escape the disruption of the Mexican Revolution. When Frank was no longer able to come into the shop, Josefina was conversant with the rare book collection. Also, Mexican customers and publishers alike found her an invaluable resource.

What makes the weekends during the war so much a part of the bookstore story is that they were an extension of the bookstore. That was the unifying factor—the shop and Florence Rosengren were the two things the regulars shared. If you were attracted to the bookstore, that said something about you. As Figgi remembered:

> There was, however, a problem. In those days, all retail businesses closed at one o'clock on Saturday afternoon; the weekend had barely begun. My parents took to closing the doors but not really closing the store—letting the guys with nowhere else to go linger an hour or two. But that really did not solve anything. Besides, my father was already ill: if he was in the store, he needed to go home and rest his

arthritic bones. If he wasn't, he was missing out on all the brilliant talk. Inevitably, first one, then another, then a few were invited to the house on Anastacia for Saturday dinner. Then they were invited for Sunday lunch. Some, invited for both, found little reason to leave between meals and would sleep in an outbuilding that was once a stable now remodeled as a studio/guest house. Just about all met new people on post they wanted to introduce to this wonderful place and so, of course, they brought them along. Florence would ask ten for Sunday lunch and down the path would come the invited one with three others.

Those in military service who had access to the PX could buy food rationed for civilians and contributed to the larder. They also helped with the yard work and other chores without being asked. And Florence's friends also took turns cooking and serving: Amy Freeman Lee, a painter and poet who had a studio in the former River Road Country Day School; Janette Sebring Lowrey, author of children's books including *The Poky Little Puppy*, a best seller in the Little Golden Books series, and *Annunciata and the Shepherds* about the miracle play, "Los Pastores," performed every Christmas season in San Antonio; Dora Davenport, with the Bexar County Juvenile Court; and Ethel Marie Moss, who had what was then an executive position with the telephone company as training supervisor for the state of Texas. Ethel remembered that she and Florence would search through recipe books for casserole dishes— "anything we could get on the ration and feed the army." A tremendous tureen of cabbage soup with Swedish meatballs bubbling on the stove all day long was a popular solution on all counts. Florence would also bake eight loaves of bread every weekend— enough to serve 20 to 30 guests.

There was a warmth and acceptance from Florence and most of the young men who frequented the Rosengren house during the war years found her enchanting. The center of their adoration, she delighted in having these discerning young people around her. Frank was much more difficult because he was in pain and could become irascible. In his frustration, he spent much of the time secluded in his office. No longer able to play or sing himself, he did not share a passion for recorded music to the degree that Florence and most of the regulars did. Sunday evenings, special recordings which Florence sought out were played for the gathering.

Pets-with-personalities were always part of the Rosengren household and were an additional source of endearment. During the war years, there was "Tick," the cat, and "Tock," a modified Boston bull dog—and the ducks who wandered up from the nearby river, attracted by the ancient water pump in the yard. The ducks were named for the Roman gods: "Minerva," goddess of Wisdom, and "Apollo," god of music and poetry. When a dozen ducklings hatched in Minerva's nest in the corner of the yard, under the yellow Confederate jasmine, it was quite the talk of the town.

Of all the "regulars," only two had been friends prior to military service: Jacques Abrams, as he was known professionally but as "Jackie" to all others, was born in Lufkin, Texas. He was living in New York City before the war, as was Daniel Schorr who grew up in the Bronx. The two attended concerts and other events together. Abrams was in a special services unit of the Air Force stationed at Randolph Field, fifteen miles northeast of San Antonio.* A classical pianist who first performed in public at age six, he debuted with the Philadelphia Orchestra at Carnegie Hall in 1937. Daniel Schorr was assigned to the Eighth Armored Division at Camp Polk, Louisiana, where "mud and mosquitoes" were his worst enemy. He was working for the Jewish Telegraphic Agency when he was drafted in late 1942.

One weekend, the two friends met in Houston where Abrams suggested, "Danny, you shouldn't be in Louisiana, you should be where I am," and Schorr replied, "You are a well-known pianist. Arrange it." And he did. Abrams revealed his plan: "The general at Randolph is a particular friend of mine. I play for his dinners. He likes me very much. All those generals know each other. I will tell him to arrange it with your general." The orders came through re-assigning Schorr as a "rare bird," that is, a person needed in a certain place, to G2, the intelligence section at Fort Sam with offices in the historic 1878 Quadrangle.

———

* In the memories of those involved—and with whom it was possible to make contact after seventy years—it was not always clear who were Army Air Forces, who were Army, or who came in the early or late years, who stayed or were shipped overseas. In the context of this story, it should be remembered that the U.S. Army Air Forces was the military aviation arm of the United States, 1941 to 1947. Before 1941 it had been the Army Air Corps; the U.S. Air Force was created in 1947. During World War II, Randolph Field was under the command of the Fourth Army with headquarters at Fort Sam Houston in San Antonio. The Eighth Armored Division was also under the Fourth Army. Hence the same chain of command.

Abrams, who had a way of speaking with enormous hyperbole, added, "There are some WONDERFUL people here that I want you to meet. Their name is Rosengren. I talked to Florence and she would be THRILLED to meet you." And indeed she was. Encouraged to do so by Florence, Schorr gathered material for an article about the rampant discrimination against Mexican-Americans in South Texas—"treated as badly as Negroes anywhere in the South." Fired by her passionate social conscience, she introduced him to a bright up-and-coming young Hispanic politician named Henry B. González as a source and contact. The piece, " 'Reconverting' Mexican Americans," was published in the *New Republic*, December 30, 1946—after his discharge from the Army and en route to Holland for his next assignment as news editor of the Netherlands News Agency. Subsequently, he joined Edward R. Murrow's CBS-TV team, and later, was a White House reporter who made Nixon's "enemy list." He ended his career as an interpreter of national and international events for National Public Radio.

As Daniel Schorr remembered, "The extrovert who took over was Halsey Davis who was also from New York. I can see where all sorts of would-be stars were very unhappy because Halsey was Florence's favorite. So funny—so much 'the Irish poet'—the young Yeats kind of thing who would read his own poetry on occasion."

All agreed that Florence doted on him, but as Figgi observed, "He was ten years her junior and she was still a Catholic girl married to this older and very unwell man—and that was that. Nothing was going to happen." [William Butler Yeats, the Irish poet and dramatist, was the primary focus of Florence's own collecting. Her Yeats collection was sold to Maggs Bros. following her death.]

Dr. Gerald Taylor was another soldier who gave solace to Florence during her husband's illness—a gentle, soothing person with a boyish eagerness about him. After serving his internship in pediatrics, he went on active duty with postings to Fort Sam Houston and other hospital units before shipping out to England early in 1944, just prior to the D-Day invasion of western Europe. Experiences as a field surgeon in a hospital near the front lines caused him to be more concerned about the mind and the spirit. He felt he would be more useful to society as a psychiatrist— and a very successful one he would be. Dr. Taylor responded to the author's inquiries

A gathering at 104 Anastacia. From the right, Halsey Davis, Frank Rosengren Sr., Ethel Moss, and Florence Rosengren. The two men on the left who shared this particular "Parnassus weekend" have not been identified. *Rosengren Family Collection.*

in February and March of 1997: "There are many things to say about Florence. From the first day I wandered into the Bookstore, we just got along and remained very close throughout the years, although there was so much geography in between. Throughout the War, she kept up the letters and packages with all sorts of goodies for the palate, mind and heart. I feel the association was of such a spiritual nature that it existed no matter what."

For the next four decades, the friends did not see each other but hardly a week passed that letters and books—treasures and treats to be shared from Gerald—were not delivered to Florence. "However, when I realized that Florence was ill, I knew it was urgent to go and see her and I was glad that I did." In an undated letter following his visit and the delivery of his recent gift of an exercise bicycle, Florence wrote: "I am very excited about the bicycle. I believe it will be a great help and the prospect of being able to bounce out of the rocker has me determined to work at it."

Beginning in 1940, prior to military service, Kent Kennan taught for two years in the College of Fine Arts, University of Texas at Austin, under Dean William Doty. Due to poor eyesight, he had difficulty entering military service. He persisted and was finally admitted but was restricted to non-combatant service as a bandsman stationed at Randolph Field. After his posting to San Antonio, he played the piano in a dance band on Iwo Jima and hoped that the Japanese knew that he was a non-combatant.

Of his relationship with the Rosengrens, he observed: "You can imagine going from an army barracks where you are sharing space with two hundred men to a beautifully-appointed house—like the world you were used to—a home away from home and a very artistic home it was."

In 1936 at age 23, Kennan was awarded the Prix de Rome, winner of the first grand prize in the musical composition category—first awarded in 1803. This allowed him to study for three years in Europe, primarily at the American Academy in Rome. His "Three Pieces for Orchestra," composed in Rome, was premiered in 1939 by the Eastman-Rochester Orchestra. Between 1936 and 1956, his compositions included works for orchestra, chamber ensemble and solo instruments. After that, he devoted himself to teaching and writing. His elder brother, George Kennan, served as ambassador to Russia in the early 1950s and would shape U.S. policy towards the Soviet Union for more than forty years.

And then there were the women who volunteered to serve in the WAVES, a unit of the U.S. Naval Reserve during the war, stationed at the Cable Censorship Office in the Post Office at the north end of Alamo Plaza. Lola Belle Curbo was the first of the WAVES to be posted to San Antonio. She arrived in April of 1943, but was soon joined by thirty others. On her first visit one Saturday morning to the Rosengren's shop in the Milam Building, she was surprised by the number of people in the shop, but also by the fact that some very personable off-duty GIs—who were knowledgeable about books—were acting as salespeople. One of her duties was to entertain the Lieutenant Commander who was in charge of the WAVES in the Third Naval District on her annual tour of inspection. Having been advised about what to expect at the Rosengrens' weekend salons—including the ignoring of her rank—she was eager to accept and had a fine time arguing with a corporal. Like all the rest, she was still a civilian at heart.

Nick Attanasio was another regular and, at war's end, Nick and Lola planned to be married at City Hall. But Florence would not hear of it and insisted on having the wedding at 104 Anastacia. The band of friends who were still in town "did the decorating, arranged the music, planned the supper and paid for it all" as their wedding presents to the couple. In addition to Daniel Schorr, there was Paul Wonner, an artist who would rise to prominence in the 1950s as an abstract expressionist painter associated with the Bay Area Figurative Movement; William Strickland, who founded and went on to conduct the Nashville Symphony from 1946 to 1951; and Burt Benedict, a "Hollywood Rich Boy" whose father was an executive at one of the major movie studios.

Another WAVE, Mimi Drayton worked for an advertising agency in Chicago after the war and handled the Hallmark account. She also published novels under the pen name of Dayton Rommel, including *Cry of Peacocks* (Dodd Mead, 1963). And there were still others who made their mark musically. Robert Wallenborn—whose contribution to the war effort was his mastery of six or seven languages—was a brilliant pianist who toured as a recitalist and served as accompanist to a number of singers, including Ezio Pinza and Blanche Thebom. He also taught piano in the Department of Music at Washington University in St. Louis. A GI named Norman Granz flung open the door of Rosengren's and cried, "My God, a bookstore. I thought I'd never see one again." Jazz at the Philharmonic (JATP) was the title of a series of jazz concerts, tours and recordings which Granz produced between 1944 and 1983. The JATP concerts were among the first high-profile performances to feature racially integrated bands, and Granz was known to cancel some bookings rather than have the musicians perform for segregated audiences in the South. Florence must have cheered him on for that. Among others whose names are at least remembered but with whom contact has been lost: journalist Lennie Darnell, who after the war became editor of the Youngstown, Ohio, *Vindicator*; writer Benji Ater and her former husband Dewitt Drury, an actor; comedian Burney Gould; and Joe Goodrich, a psychologist.

Then there were various celebrity-types around too briefly to become "regulars" but who surely enlivened the scene: Gail Kubik, a composer who was doing film scores for the First Motion Picture Unit of the U.S. Army Air Forces, such as "The Memphis Belle" (1944); and Dimitri Kessel, war correspondent and combat photographer, who was brought by Holland McCombs, Southwest bureau chief for Time Inc.

With Allied victories and the end of the war in the summer of 1945, so ended the Parnassus weekends. As Kent Kennan remembered: "The whole reason why people congregated at the Rosengrens' house [was] because Frank could not get out. It is poignant that his disability was the cause of such happy gatherings." The happy scene was fading. Figgi enlisted in the Army Air Forces following his graduation from Jefferson High School in 1944, and Frank Sr.'s condition worsened. Finally, it became necessary for him to go into a nursing home in 1947, where he died in 1949.

This was the end of an era and Frank Rosengren is best remembered as Amy Freeman Lee recalled her first encounter with him in the shop soon after it opened on the sixth floor of the Milam Building: "I always smile when I think of him. He had the bushiest eyebrows of anybody I can ever remember—sort of like a cliff-hanging balcony—and a mustache. Reminded me of Mark Twain in a way—kind of rosy cheeks and very bright burning eyes that looked right through you. He was very jolly and warm and made you feel comfortable."

As the mid-century mark approached, the future beckoned. After military service, Figgi followed in his mother's footsteps and entered the University of Chicago—commuting from Whiting where he lived with his Kednay grandparents. Ethel Moss was invited by Florence to live at 104 Anastacia where she would occupy the spacious, well-appointed front bedroom—now the guest room—until she was transferred to Dallas. Florence moved into "the Catholic cell"—modest even by monastic standards.

While the Rosengren "regulars" scattered the world over in pursuit of their chosen life's work—often with stellar success—correspondence sustained the relationships. Florence was usually at the shop by 5 a.m. seven days a week in order to clear her in-box using the typewriter she favored. And for the rest of her life, she kept a file box of letters that were most precious close at hand. The collection includes: hundreds of letters from Gerald Taylor from 1944 to 1988, including his wartime experiences; sixty-four letters from Paul Wonner from 1946 to 1984; Kent Kennan, the first in 1945 from Iwo Jima, until 1987; as well as significant numbers from Halsey Davis, Robert Wallenborn, Jacques Abrams and, of course, Daniel Schorr from the Hague, Moscow, and all points east and west.

Another collection of letters between the Rosengrens and folklorist J. Frank Dobie survives in the Harry Ransom Humanities Research Center of the University of Texas—three dozen letters, the first dating from 1940—often planning his frequent visits to the bookstore. Dobie's purpose in life was to show the people of Texas and the Southwest the richness of their culture and their traditions. In response to her interest, he advised Florence about the doings of the Texas Folklore Society and the Texas Institute of Letters and recommended books on the subject which she dutifully read. In a letter of December 27, 1944, from the senior Rosengren to Dobie—beginning with the salutation "Pancho amigo"—he wrote:

> Our son will be inducted shortly no doubt. When he comes back, we want him to go to the University of Texas but not if it is dominated by the present Regents and the political scum that support them. . . . That university fight has got to be won, somehow. Boy, am I becoming a Texan. Now I want to fight.

The University of Texas regents, critical of the university's liberal professors, had fired President Homer P. Rainey in November 1944. Dobie, a liberal Democrat, was outraged and vociferous . . . and the regents soon found a way to dismiss him from the UT faculty on which he had served off and on since 1914.

7

Evictions

and Propitious Moves

Widowed at 44, Florence Rosengren was thereafter married to the bookstore—playing the role she assigned herself: making others feel important, making them feel intelligent.[1] Figgi had graduated from the University of Chicago with a bachelor's degree in liberal arts, and now had work assignments in Mexico and elsewhere. Along the way he met Camille Sweeney—introduced by Florence, of course. After Figgi and Cam were married, there was an empty nest at home for Florence.

Then, after fifteen years in the Milam Building as one of San Antonio's most valued cultural amenities, seeming disaster struck. Rosengren's Books was evicted when an adjoining business, the Travis Building and Loan Association at 111 West Travis Street, needed space for expansion. Florence's optimistic spirit must have been challenged, but help was at hand.

Walter Loughridge, who had been Harry Hertzberg's protégé and law partner, became the Rosengrens' legal advisor after Hertzberg's death in 1940. Ever helpful, he would continue to advise Florence about business and legal matters for several decades more.[2] Also willing to lend a hand was Rawlings "Rolly" Hamilton—a practical and versatile man, knowledgeable about literary esoterica and a devotee of Florence. Rolly located a vacant space that had formerly been a bus station and convinced the owners to rent the half of the property facing Travis Park—and the St. Anthony Hotel beyond—for the new Rosengren's. The address was 305 East Pecan.[3] The vibrant center of San Antonio in the 1950s, the location was rich in history. St. Mark's Episcopal Church adjoined to the east. Designed in 1875 by Richard Upjohn, one of the foremost church architects of the nineteenth century, the beautiful church featured one of the city's best organs and was the site of many concerts.

Before World War II, Rolly Hamilton had worked as program director at radio station KBAC in the Milam Building and was frequently in Rosengren's. He also designed sets for the San Antonio Little Theater and directed plays for the Temple Beth-El Players and the Catholic Theater Guild. He had spent one year in the military and was in the "ready reserve"—subject to immediate call-up. Rolly worked in the store for four months before December 7, 1941, when he returned to active duty.

Rolly was assigned to the U.S. Army's map command, stationed mainly on Guam, where he drew maps for use in the Pacific theater. Jo Mielziner, a theatrical scenic and lighting designer who later became the most successful set designer of the "Golden Era of Broadway," was on his staff. Rolly's naval liaison was a young lieutenant named Henry Fonda. At war's end, Mielziner encouraged Rolly to become his partner in New York, but Rolly returned to San Antonio where he was committed to raising his younger brother, Richard, following the death of their parents. Rolly resumed his theater activities and

Rawlings "Rolly" Hamilton, 1951. Before World War II, Rolly had directed local plays, including a 1938 production of Emmet Lavery's "First Legion," which included a 12-year-old Figgi Rosengren in the cast. Hamilton was the business manager of the original San Antonio Symphony Orchestra. He worked at Rosengren's for a few months in 1941, and returned to the store soon after the conclusion of the war. In 1951, when the store moved from the Milam Building to Travis Park, Rolly found and negotiated the new location, designed the new store—with a theatrical flair—and even built custom bookshelves. Rolly later helped adapt the shelves for the move to 312 Bonham Street in 1959, which he also designed. A few of his original shelves even made it to the final location on Losoya Street.

worked part-time at the bookstore for years.

With an abundance of taste and talent but no professional architectural training, Rolly nevertheless designed the new store, acting as building contractor and occasional carpenter as well. A true jack-of-all-trades, he created a two-story space with an upper gallery on the diagonal, accessed by a perpendicular metal stair. The upper gallery was mainly dedicated to rare recordings as well as artist's prints—limited editions of woodcuts, lithographs, intaglio and the like. At this time, Florence represented the Associated American Artists whose head, Sylvan Cole, had been stationed in San Antonio during the war years and surely knew the Rosengrens. Rolly liked being in the bookstore—liked waiting on people—visiting. He was less interested in the business part of the operation. He would say "she gripes about how hard she works, but you try to get your fingers in the pie and you'll get slapped real quick." Florence often remarked that Rolly was her good right hand, as was Sue Shields who had arrived in the late 1940s as a bookkeeper. Soon Sue too was multi-tasking as both bookkeeper and manager of the children's section.

The bookstore would now be at the epicenter of one of the major conservation battles of the 1950s. The land for Travis Park had been the orchard of Samuel Maverick, who willed the site to the city in 1870. In 1954, the park was threatened when a local businessman planned the construction and operation of a subterranean parking facility under this early municipal park. The San Antonio Conservation Society and other civic groups blocked alteration of the park—and where better to meet and strategize than at the bookstore? The issue was finally resolved in 1957 by the Texas Supreme Court.[4]

Rolly Hamilton and Ethel Marie Moss, late 1940s, probably on Houston Street. A good friend of Florence, Ethel appears in numerous photographs. She reportedly "adored" Rolly, though they were never a couple.

The 1950s were a euphoric time when it seemed that the cultural cosmos would find its balance—in spite of the wars in southeast Asia. A new day dawned and Rosengren's on Travis Park became San Antonio's "literary clubhouse." Stimulating ideas were discussed at spontaneous gatherings when cosmopolitan newcomers joined the Milam Building regulars. Robert Lynn Batts Tobin started going to Rosengren's in the Milam Building in 1944 when he was ten years old.[5] After his twice weekly visits to the orthodontist to have his braces tightened—which he endured for eight years—he was allowed to select a book as reward. He remembered that "Florence had a tremendous influence in knowing my mind and she tried subtly to improve it. I passed through the Alamo Heights schools but my education was more at Rosengren's." He added that his love of books was also inherited from his family—a "whole line of bibliomaniacs."

In 1954, when Robert was 19 and a sophomore at the University of Texas at Austin, his father, Edgar Tobin, and aviation pioneer Thomas Braniff were killed in a plane crash in Louisiana. At the time, Tobin Aerial Survey was the largest map-maker for the oil industry in the country. Robert withdrew from the university and took over the business, which he would lead through unprecedented growth. In the decades to come, he would be an active participant in the diverse philanthropies he supported, eventually funding (with his mother) the Tobin Wing of the Marion Koogler McNay Art Museum.

John Palmer Leeper was named founding director of the McNay museum following Mrs. McNay's death in 1950, and he would serve in that capacity until 1991. In her bequest, Mrs. McNay gave the City of San Antonio her home—a Spanish Colonial Revival mansion on acreage called Sunset Hills, at the intersection of Austin Highway and New Braunfels Avenue. Designed by Atlee B. and Robert M. Ayres and built in 1927, the structure housed her collection of works of art in the Expressionist tradition. The museum opened to the public in 1954. John Leeper had been a student in Paul Sachs' course in museum curatorship at the Fogg Art Museum at Harvard.[6] It was at Harvard that he met his future wife, Blanche Magurn, who was studying Chinese porcelain with a scholar on the faculty. At the time, Blanche's sister, Ruth, worked in the prints and drawings department at the Fogg. The McNay's print collection would later be organized on the Fogg model. Before the Leepers moved to San Antonio, he worked in the curatorial department of the Corcoran Museum in Washington, D.C. and as director of the Pasadena Art Institute. Poet and painter Amy Freeman Lee, whose works were handled by the Dalzell Hatfield Galleries in Los Angeles, became acquainted with the Leepers in California and saw to it that they met Florence Rosengren and other like-minded souls upon their arrival in San Antonio.[7]

John Leeper's accomplishments were prodigious in amplifying Mrs. McNay's art collection as well as in the development of the museum library. In this, Florence Rosengren was an active participant, as was Blanche Leeper, who would serve as head librarian. Leeper stated: "We formulated a direction. There had to be a solid text . . . no picture books . . . texts that provided answers to general questions about art in world history as well as specific questions about works in our collection in order to expedite original research." When the library was in its infancy,

Florence would special order encyclopedias of art history as well as extraordinary books in the fine arts that no one else would buy except Robert Tobin and the McNay.[8]

John Leeper told a revealing story about Robert and the move in 1984 into the new two-story Tobin Wing, designed by Ford, Powell & Carson, and given by Robert's mother, Margaret Batts Tobin. "We transported the entire library—26,000 books— in grocery carts borrowed from Charlie Butt. They were already cataloged and just needed to be shelved. When we finished, I said 'Robert, for god's sake, stop buying books.' He said 'No. Let's build more libraries.'"

Florence and Frank Duane Rosengren also made a significant gift in memory of the late Frank Sr. to the Prints and Drawings Collection at the McNay—prints from the Associated American Artists series. The first gift in 1969 included 28 prints. An additional 41 were donated in 1971. Florence was also cited as a donor supplying missing numbers in periodical files as well as museum publications.[9]

Alas, business stability was not among the Rosengren's awards for their civic virtues. After just seven years at the Travis Park location, in 1957, Rosengren's Books was evicted once more—forced out by their neighbor, First Federal Savings and Loan Association, which needed space for expansion. Florence was now confronted with finding yet another new location within the bookstore's budget. Rolly Hamilton once more scouted out an excellent space—smaller but commercially much superior. It was on the ground floor of the Crockett Hotel, facing the rear grounds of the Alamo. The address was first listed as being on Nacogdoches Road, which once led to the east Texas town of the same name. The name of the short stretch of road behind the Alamo was then changed to Bonham—after James Bonham, a hero of the Battle of the Alamo. For the next 25 years, the address of the shop would be 312 Bonham. Here was the store that would soon be proclaimed by author and *Harper's Magazine* editor Willie Morris as "one of the finest and most admirable bookstores in America."

It was a blessing that Florence's optimism was unfailing, as moving a bookstore is a difficult task. Still, she could always find solace in a good book—as she described in a letter early in 1958 to J. Frank Dobie:

> I've never worked as hard in my life as I have in the last four months and I am weary, weary, weary. But at night after I've finished the things I have to do, I make a good rum drink, get in a nightgown and robe and curl up on the couch and read—sometimes from *The Longhorns*, sometimes from *Tales of the Mustang* for the past week. It has been a happy time with one of your several books and I have wanted to send you a note to say again how much they mean to me—and you mean to me.[10]

Camille Sweeney and
Frank Duane Rosengren

Camille Sweeney was San Antonio's own version of *Eloise at the Plaza*. Emmett Sweeney, her father, was a graduate of Cornell University, an attorney and the founder of Guaranty Abstract Title Company, which was located in the Milam Building. Her mother, Georgette Lodovic, was a member of a significant South Texas family. "Cam," as she was known, was born in New York but the family soon moved back to Texas. The Sweeneys lived in the historic Menger Hotel for three years beginning in 1935. Their suite faced Alamo Plaza with a night view of the neon-illuminated "Cowboy Roping Cattle" on the façade of Joske's Department Store. Then for thirteen years—from age eight until Cam married at twenty-one—the family lived at the St. Anthony Hotel, the playground of stars of the silver screen as well as world leaders. Cam would occasionally find herself riding the elevator with the likes of John Wayne, Veronica Lake—famous for her *femme fatale* roles during the 1940s—or even Eleanor Roosevelt.

When Frank Duane and Cam met, she was working on her master's degree in library science at Our Lady of the Lake University. She had been a frequent customer at the bookstore for most of her life and was well known to Florence, but had never met Figgi, who had been living in Mexico City since he finished a short stint in the military.

One day in the fall of 1950, Rolly and Florence found themselves short-staffed for a book signing by Newbery Award recipient Lois Lenski.

They asked Cam to help out. After the signing, Rolly invited Cam back to River Road for dinner. (Rolly was renting one of Florence's cottages there. Among his numerous skills, Rolly was an excellent cook.) That was when Cam met Figgi. The rather bookish couple's first date was the next evening, when they saw Orson Welles' film *Macbeth*. Frank Duane and Camille wed on January 13, 1951. Later that year, Margo Jones would produce one of Frank's first plays, "Walls Rise Up," at Theater 51 in Dallas. The play was optioned by Broadway, and a new chapter began.

The couple soon moved to New York where Frank became a staff writer on the CBS television series "Omnibus." (Figgi and Cam's departure for New York was celebrated by popular San Antonio cartoonist Jack Kent in his "King Aroo" strip. Since the strip was syndicated nationally, it was some send-off. Kent, also a prolific children's author, spent untold hours in the store.)

Florence's only grandchild, Emily, was born the first month after Figgi and Cam arrived in New York. She would attend the Rudolf Steiner School, a Waldorf School where "learning is a joyous activity." The Waldorf School's philosophy was similar to that which inspired the River Road Country Day School her father had attended. They learned the joys of weekend commuting in 1955-1956, when Figgi took an RCA-NBC Fellowship in Drama, and became "Playwright-in-Residence" at Yale University. Back in New York, Camille was now on the curatorial staff at the Metropolitan Museum of Art, where she worked on the museum's Bulletin when she was not cataloging the Herzfeld Arabic Manuscript collection.

Cam and Figgi returned to San Antonio in 1961. Emily, now ten years old, attended the Keystone School before enrolling in Incarnate Word High School and College, where dramatics were her consuming interest.

In the 1960s, during the years leading up to San Antonio's world's fair, HemisFair '68, Frank Duane was a consultant, producer and writer for numerous projects associated with the fair.[11] The newly constructed Institute of Texan Cultures—a centerpiece of HemisFair '68—had only one female on its senior staff, Cam Rosengren. Cam helped to acquire, catalog and maintain the original artifact collection.

Cam continued to work for the Institute after the conclusion of HemisFair '68, while Frank continued to write plays, screenplays, and television scripts, plus maintaining a column in both the *San Antonio Light* and the *North San Antonio Times* and serving as an executive producer for KLRN-TV. Neither Frank nor Cam particularly wanted to run the bookstore, but it was difficult not to be pulled into its orbit. When Florence began to talk of retiring (she never formally "retired"), it was clear that Cam was the best qualified person to accept the mantle. She began daily management of the store in 1979.

8

Common Cause

Florence Rosengren possessed a genius for matching people and books but also for matching people with people who shared common interests. In terms of "waves still breaking on distant shores," there is no better example than her collaboration with Frank Wardlaw, who founded the University of Texas Press in 1950 and the Texas A&M University Press in 1974—having earlier founded the University of South Carolina Press in 1945. In a letter of February 14, 1977, to Florence Rosengren, Frank Wardlaw wrote:

> I am sure you recall the details of the establishment of the Elma Dill Russell Spencer series at the University of Texas Press. I had discovered Mary Motz Wills' fine wildflower paintings at the Texas Memorial Museum and wanted to enlist the aid of a botanist to develop a guide to the more common wildflowers of the state. You introduced me to Elma Dill Spencer and she gave the University $30,000 to establish a revolving fund out of which *The Roadside Flowers of Texas* was published. When I left the University of Texas, not only had there been six printings of *The Roadside Flowers of Texas* but six other books had been published out of this fund—including such titles as *Painted Walls of Mexico*, *The Cacti of the Southwest*, *Sea Shells of the Texas Coast*, and *Theodore Gentilz*:

Artist of the Old Southwest. When I left Austin in 1974 there was over $40,000 in the fund. You will recall the great pleasure Elma Dill derived from the development of these books. We became fast friends in the course of this common endeavor.[1]

The Roadside Flowers of Texas—still a bestseller for the press in 2014—was first published in 1961. Close on its heels, Wardlaw had another series in mind for the UT Press: books about "Texas Range Life." Florence knew of another benefactor, perfect for such a series—Montagu Kingsmill Brown. London-born Brown had been sent to Texas in 1903 to work for the English syndicate that owned the Francklyn Land and Cattle Company in the Texas Panhandle. Now he was an elderly, very well-off "bachelor cowboy" with investments in cattle, wheat and oil who wintered in San Antonio.[2] Every morning, he would walk from the Aurora Apartments in the Tobin Hill neighborhood, just north of downtown, to Rosengren's Books to visit and make purchases. Despite his wealth, Brown lived frugally. However, when Florence broached the idea of his supporting a publication fund, he responded and endowed the M. K. Brown Series. *Six Thousand Miles of Fence: Life on the XIT Ranch of Texas,* by Cordelia Sloan Duke, widow of the ranch manager of one of the English-owned ranches in the Texas Panhandle, and co-authored by Joe Bertram Frantz, came out in 1961. The second book in the series, *Francklyn Land and Cattle Company: A Panhandle Enterprise 1882-1957,* by Lester Fields Sheffy, was published in 1963. Brown, who died in 1964, would have taken pleasure in the many future fruits of his generosity.

According to Henry C. Dethloff, writing in 1999: "Walter Prescott Webb, J. Frank Dobie, and Roy Bedicek played major roles in Wardlaw's life and that of the University of Texas Press. Within two decades, the press had become one of the nation's leading regional university publishing houses [by publishing] books focused on Texas, the southwest and Latin America." However, "some critics found Wardlaw's apparent preoccupation with Texas and regional topics parochial and called the press the 'cow chip press'." Faculty members thought the university press should focus more on truly intellectual issues and topics.[3] Within a few years of retirement, Wardlaw decided it was time for a change. Professor Dethloff also described the role of Texas Aggie alumnus John H. Lindsey and others in the evolution of the Texas A&M University Press and of Frank Wardlaw's contributions as founding director. To continue from Wardlaw's 1977 letter to Florence:

> Now for my new press at Texas A&M, I am seeking similar support for a series of beautiful books on various aspects of the Texas environment. The first book in the series would be a photographic book on Texas wildlife —mammals, birds, fish, amphibians, and reptiles—to be derived principally from the files of *Texas Parks & Wildlife Magazine*. . . . Such a book would bring pride to all Texans and would quicken the interest of many in their heritage from the natural world and their desire to conserve it. . . . This book would cost between $40,000 and $50,000 to produce. . . . I am wondering if you know of any well-to-do Texan interested in our natural heritage who

might be able to make a gift to Texas A&M University for the book described above. Such a gift would constitute a revolving fund out of which other beautiful books devoted to the environment and the preservation of our heritage would eventually be published.

Florence's friend, Louise Lindsey Merrick of Tyler, Texas, was a perfect match. She was in the process of donating her 5,400-acre Merrick Bar-O Ranch, located in Bandera and Medina Counties, to the Texas Parks and Wildlife Department—with the stipulation that it "be kept far removed and untouched by modern civilization, where everything is preserved intact, yet put to a useful purpose." (Five years later, the Hill Country State Natural Area opened to the public.) Mrs. Merrick provided a $50,000 endowment in 1977 to establish the Louise Lindsey Merrick Natural Environment Series, which is still active in 2014. *Texas Wildlife: Photographs from Texas Parks & Wildlife Magazine* would be the first book in the series, the result of a cooperative effort between the university's wildlife science department and the magazine. In Louise Merrick's letter to Frank Wardlaw of March 9, 1978, following the book's publication, she wrote: "Thank you for this book but do not send me any more copies as I've ordered four from Florence. I want to start the buying public off right and help Florence too."

Elma Dill Russell Spencer's earlier collaboration with Wardlaw at the University of Texas Press had been so rewarding that her foundation decided to endow, posthumously, a second series at his new press at Texas A&M University: "Essays on the American West."

The role of the "publisher's rep" as the liaison between publishers and bookstores is noted in Chapter Five, but a closer relationship between Florence and Alfred Knopf is documented in the Knopf papers archived in the Harry Ransom Humanities Research Center at the University of Texas at Austin. In her letter to Knopf dated July 11, 1956, she wrote concerning *Fifty Years,* one his recent publications: "I was nineteen years old when I married Frank and shortly after that I met you in the bookshop [in Chicago]. In October of this year, I will be sixty—so you see that much of your *Fifty Years* directly concerns me and is especially meaningful." Later in a letter dated June 30, 1976, she wrote: "You are 'Mr. Publisher' and have been for so many years. The kind of bookshop I run has been much influenced by you. The *Texas Monthly* listed us in the current issue (July) as the best bookshop in the state and much of the honor belongs to you."

There is also correspondence from the early 1950s in the Knopf papers between Florence and Herbert Weinstock, executive editor of the publishing house, who solicited her recommendations for publishable manuscripts. Florence put her friend, Janette Sebring Lowrey, in touch with the juvenile editor at Knopf, but nothing came of that contact.[4]

In her letter of August 21, 1953, Florence wrote: "John Igo tells me that he has sent some of his work to you. He is a young man of considerable talent whom I have known since he was a little boy." Weinstock replied "there is nothing we could publish though it shows earnestness and intelligence." Florence could "read" people and John Igo's earnestness and intelligence were already evident at 15, while a student at Edison High School.[5] Grace Wright, whom Igo deemed "one of the greatest school librarians of all times," had chosen him as one of her student assistants. The year was 1942 and Rosengren's in the Milam Building was the destination for one of the educational field trips she planned for her assistants. Later, while a freshman at Trinity University—then still at a temporary campus on Woodlawn Avenue—Igo became a regular. Until the day the store closed, John Igo would be in Rosengren's at least weekly. He was soon one of the inner circle—all liberal-minded and on the same wave length—almost an extended family that cut across social castes, money, and race. There was no common denominator but self-selection among Florence's friends. She knew how to match up people and how to mobilize them when the need arose. When she would send out the call, the gang would gather, especially when distinguished literati visited the shop. She would then invite them to return for apples and tea. When political action was required, as when Fay Sinkin was fighting a battle over water quality, the bookstore friends mobilized to help.

Florence's genius for matching up people was more than matched by her conviction that "people who want books and books who want people should get together." Florence never lost her love of the "seredipitous find" and was well aware that leaving a book that had become rare on the shelf—at its original price—allowed others to enjoy that sense of discovery. One day, a book salesman in the shop pulled a volume by Tennessee Williams off the shelf and said, "Seven dollars and fifty cents? That's not enough. . . . In Dallas or Houston or Denver or Chicago, these things sell for fifty dollars." She answered, "That is a long way to travel to pay more."

Then there was the charm of simple generosity. One of the treasures in the rare bookcase in the shop on Bonham Street was a volume by English poet Thomas Chatterton, published in 1794 and in its original binding. The price of $50 was far more than John Igo could afford at the time. Still, he would carefully examine it without comment. As he remembered: "One day, I came in and she said 'this is for you' and gave me the book. 'Yes, it belongs to you. It has been sitting here all this time and no one else has ever touched it. You should have it.'"

Of all John Igo's accomplishments—as an educator and the recipient of several teaching excellence awards, and as an author, critic and civic leader—there are two that Florence Rosengren would have found most gratifying.[6] In the 1980s, he received the Grothaus Medallion for distinguished service to area libraries—the only non-librarian ever to receive this honor. Julia Ellen Grothaus was the director of the San Antonio Public Library system from 1933 to 1957, with whom Florence had worked closely, beginning in 1936. Then in December of 2007, the John Igo Branch Library in the San Antonio Public Library system opened at 13330 Kyle Seale Parkway. Igo credits Florence thusly. "She was Virgil to my Dante in the *Inferno*. She led very quietly—off-hand and ladylike, but with a devilish twinkle."

Rosengren's Books, 312 Bonham Street, directly behind the Alamo, on the bottom floor of the
Crockett Hotel. April 12, 1982. Located here for
a quarter of a century, 1957 to 1982, this shop was
frequented by writers like Larry McMurtry, George
Sessions Perry, John Graves, William Goyen, Joe B.
Frantz, Lon Tinkle, Walter Lord, Willie Morris,
among many others. J. Frank Dobie was one of
the Texas writers who had book signing parties in
all four store locations. Sometimes a weekly visitor, Dobie once inscribed a book to his "cherished
friend" Florence: "After I have written a book, I
wish I hadn't, were it not for the cheerios from
you. . . . Whenever I come to see you, I want to
write another. You give me good medicine."

9

Small Spaces, Expansive Ideas

Rosengren's Bookstore moved to 312 Bonham Street across from the Alamo grounds in 1957. Amy Freeman Lee observed that it was an extraordinary kind of place where people who cared about books came together to exchange ideas, calling to mind Aldous Huxley's phrase, "a green oasis in the chaos of it all." It was a haven—a small space but somehow the ideas were so expansive that you did not notice.[1] Historian Joe B. Frantz recalled it as "a vigorous island of culture."

As always, the people who really cared about books came from distant and not so distant places: Louise Lindsey Merrick from Tyler in East Texas, Montagu Brown from the Panhandle and, from Corpus Christi, Mary Elizabeth Holdsworth Butt. She and her husband, Howard E. Butt, founded the H.E. Butt Foundation which was one of the earliest philanthropic foundations in Texas to fund the expansion of library services. In 1968, the Butts were awarded the Texas Library Association's Philanthropic Award in recognition of their service to libraries. Also from Corpus Christi, newspaperman Ed Harte and his wife Janet were Rosengren regulars.[2]

The director of the McNay Art Museum, John Leeper, and arts patron, Robert Tobin, were daily visitors to Rosengren's. They frequently met for lunch at the Patio Club, a "bottle club" in the historic Menger Hotel across the street from the book store. The gathering of nimble-witted friends also included: architect O'Neil Ford; city planner Sam Zisman; Joe Salek, director of the San Antonio Little Theater; and businessmen like Cam's father, Emmett Sweeney. After lunch, they would reconvene at Rosengren's, which was just across the street.

It was Maury Maverick Jr. who perhaps best defined the ineffable aura of the place:

> Rosengren's was not a neutral place about politics, but neither was it hard line liberal or conservative, Democrat or Republican. San Antonio's leading liberals and conservatives felt equally at ease there because of the charm of Florence Rosengren. It was simply a civilized hangout. She had a presence about her that created trust in her customers. . . . Her maiden name was Kednay. She was not "professional Irish," but she had an Irish something about her that grabbed your heart in serious concern one minute and made you laugh the next. Now and then I would see Frates Seeligson, wealthy San Antonio businessman, rancher, and convert to the Republican party in Rosengren's. It was obvious he liked Florence. We even liked each other as long as she was in the same room. The lady was magic.[3]

Once, when asked his Christmas wish—with all the world from which to chose—Frates Seeligson asked for a year's open account at Rosengren's—and he relished using it. When Ramona, the daughter of his brother and sister-in-law, Arthur and Linda Nixon Seeligson, married Lee Bass, the son of Perry and Nancy Lee Bass, each bridesmaid received a discriminating selection of art books from Rosengren's.

In 1959, the city fathers of San Antonio embarked on an ambitious enterprise to commemorate the upcoming 250th anniversary of its founding—the first officially designated international exposition in the Southwestern United States, HemisFair '68.[4] The site selected for the fairgrounds was on the southeastern edge of the central business district. What was then deemed an urban renewal project had been the Polish quarter around St. Michael's Catholic Church. Families who had lived in the locale for at least four generations were now displaced. O'Neil Ford was named primary architect for the planning group but in 1966, he was released from his contract, probably because of his plan to save 120 historic structures on the site. (Twenty-two historic structures were saved.) But there were other pragmatic reasons. Ford's liberal friends, whom he termed the "Leeper Colony," were the Heroes and those who did not support him and disparaged him as "that hippy architect" were the Vulgarians. Only the fair's cultural events generated by Robert Tobin met with Ford's approval, such as the full scale production of Guiseppe Verdi's opera, *Don Carlos,* or performances by Russia's famed Bolshoi Ballet.

In spite of the tragedies that plagued the decade of the 1960s, the fair opened on schedule on April 6, 1968, and ran through October 6 of the same year, attracting 6.3 million visitors. Although the fair site was not far from the bookstore, no effort was made to cater to the interests of tourists and it was business as usual. In the post-HemisFair years, the only lively activity in the downtown area were enterprises that did cater to the needs of tourists. The heart of the city as a place where San Antonians came together by chance or by design gradually ceased to exist.

While the hardiest of bibliophiles might brave Norman Brock's musty and cavernous used book store on Commerce Street, by the 1970s, Rosengren's Books alone had survived as a magnet that drew the intelligentsia to downtown.

A newcomer who found his way to Rosengren's was future mayor Phillip Hardberger—"Phil" to almost everyone—who moved to San Antonio with his family in 1970 after almost a decade in Washington serving in the administrations of two presidents.[5] As the first step in making a new start, he converted a former barbershop into the office of his law practice. Although it was a good walk from his office near the Bexar County Courthouse on Main Plaza to Rosengren's, work was slow and he spent an extended lunch hour there several times a week. He would also go down on Saturdays—"a good place to talk books and thoughts with people." His favorite spot was a quiet nook near the front door "with a very good sitting chair—good light—and you could look out at the Alamo and see people passing by. And there was always a fresh cup of coffee near at hand." He observed that "Florence crossed the bridge between a commercial establishment and the home. It was like you were in her home. You had a place to go where you were always welcome. It was my introduction to San Antonio. I met a lot of people and, by my lights, the kind of people I wanted to meet—a liberal hangout." The conservative Republicans who were the store's most affluent customers had other places to socialize with their like-minded friends.

Linda Hardberger, later the founding curator of the Tobin Collection of Theatre Arts at the McNay, tried to stay away from the bookstore because their book-buying budget was overextended—but there was an exception: Rosengren's was the only place in the city that carried the very best in children's literature. Sue Shields was the store's children's literature specialist and a beloved storyteller. The Hardbergers credit Sue with practically raising their daughter, Amy. Florence also helped the family find the perfect house, not too surprisingly on the corner of River Road and Anastacia—built by Robert Steelesmith and responsive to the architecture of what had been the River Road Country Day School next door.

Having learned much of what he knew about San Antonio at Rosengren's, Phil Hardberger would make major contributions to restoring the vitality of downtown three decades later when he was elected mayor. Among his many accomplishments during his two terms in office, from 2005 to 2009, he led efforts to double the length of the San Antonio River Walk with the opening of the Museum Reach in May of 2009, with links to the San Antonio Museum of Art and the Pearl Brewery redevelopment. A year earlier, he had been responsible for the restoration of Main Plaza, the city's original downtown center of government, enhancing its connection to the River Walk. In 2010, Main Plaza was named one of the ten "Great Public Spaces in the United States."

With all the right qualifications and experience, and a tremendous determination to keep the store alive in an era that saw the death of 90 percent of the independent book stores in the country, Camille assumed responsibility for the early-to-late, seven-days-a-week job, keeping the store in the Rosengren family. In 1980, in celebration of Florence Rosengren's seventy-fifth birthday, her son and daughter-in-law staged a surprise party at the Red Carpet, a downtown club long frequented by Cam's father. It was an elegant affair for twenty guests. Robert Tobin—the boy who preferred a book from Rosengren's after his visit to the dentist rather than an ice cream treat—declined the invitation but sent a check for one thousand dollars. His message was "buy something you really want." As her thank you gesture, Florence was true to form and sent an addition to his Irish collection—a first edition of Sean O'Casey's earliest pamphlet, published under another name and valued conservatively at twice the value of Tobin's gift.

Part-time workers, Jacque Van Norturick (left) and Nicki Beaudoin, covering books in the children's area, 1982. Water leaks the final few years at the Bonham Street location required that the books be covered in plastic every evening. The situation only got worse when the Crockett Hotel's restoration began. Nicki became the assistant manager after the store's final move to Losoya Street.

10

The Final Chapter

Located in downtown San Antonio since 1935, Rosengren's Books had become a part of the image of the ancient town: a store cherished by South Texans and sought out by visitors from around the world. By the 1970s, downtown had become Anywhere USA, and would remain so until the tragic misdirection was reversed by civic leaders at the turn of the century.

When a suitable satellite location for the bookstore would materialize, Camille Rosengren, the shop's new proprietor, would grow hopeful. H.R. Higgins Books at 5208 Broadway in Alamo Heights, a township on the near north side of San Antonio, was on the market, and reasonable offers were presented to Rosengren's. However, nothing came of these overtures because Florence Rosengren was adamant about maintaining the downtown location. It was her life. She and the store were one.[1]

The bookstore had always occupied a downtown location. In the early 1920s, Frank Rosengren Books first opened for business in Chicago in a ground-floor apartment. Later in 1925, Florence Kednay, then a student at the University of Chicago, met her future husband in his shop in the Tree Studio Building, the best of his several locations in the Windy City. After the move to San Antonio in 1935, downtown locations had thriven even after two evictions. Camille and Frank Duane determined that they had no choice but to stay downtown because this was what Florence wanted. That she was now afflicted with Parkinson's disease was also a critical factor in their decision.

In 1982, after 25 years as a star tenant at the Bonham Street address, disaster struck again when the Crockett Hotel was sold to Principal Properties, a Canadian developer. Their vice-president, Lynn Bell, assured the Rosengrens that the bookstore would be included in the corporation's plans for the renovation of the historic hotel. Cam was convinced that the firm of Ford, Powell & Carson would be the best architects for the job, so she arranged another dinner party at the Red Carpet, where she introduced the developer to O'Neil Ford. Ford also promised that the bookstore would "always be there" but Ford was no longer the decision-maker in his firm and had only a few months to live. When things went wrong, Ford was no longer able to "give 'em Hell" as he surely would have done.

The property flipped again with Dale Schuette as the ultimate owner. In Jan Jarboe's column in the *San Antonio Express-News*, the fate of the bookstore unfolds under the headline "Bookstore Boot Shabby Shame."[2] She noted that "the most recent owner is not a foreigner but a San Antonian. . . . If Schuette had gone all the way to Outer Mongolia, he could not have found a more prestigious tenant than Rosengren's Bookstore." Instead of capitalizing on Rosengren's reputation, Schuette sent the family a four-paragraph letter on the first day of April telling them to vacate immediately. The renovation plans drawn up by the architects indicated that the space previously occupied by the bookstore would be meeting rooms and a bar. Jarboe concludes: "Now a San Antonian's first step in bringing new life to the old Crockett Hotel is to evict his only blue chip tenant. We San Antonians really ought to handle our institutions with greater care."

The new owners told the Rosengrens that "they would try to give them time to move but would make no promises." Less than two weeks later, construction dust polluted the air in the shop—harmful to both people and books—and made doing business almost impossible.

Florence with Ronnie Dugger, May 13, 1982. The store had a "carry it away" sale combined with a marathon book signing party for Dugger's newly published *The Politician*. Great liberals like Dugger and Maury Maverick Jr. stood shoulder to shoulder with Texas conservatives like T.R. Fehrenbach and Frates Seeligson. Some university professors cancelled classes for the day, so that their students could witness the end of an era.

The final book signing in the Bonham Street store occurred on May 13, 1982. It honored the Rosengrens' long-time friend, Ronnie Dugger, and his latest book, *The Politician: The Life and Times of Lyndon Johnson: The Drive for Power from the Frontier to Master of the Senate*, published by W.W. Norton. Five hundred guests had come from near and far for the party. They were being served white wine and cheese nibbles and had spilled out into the street. Adding insult to injury, they were showered with dust and debris from bulldozers excavating at the back door and a Bobcat knocking down walls above. It was, indeed, a memorable "last party."

A hero finally arrived to save the day. Hap Veltman, one of three enlightened partners who owned properties along the Paseo del Rio, offered a timely solution—one that would expedite the move and was right for an independent bookstore. Waldenbooks at 223 Losoya had recently gone out of business. Cam negotiated with Jerry Sullivan, a Waldenbook's executive in New York, who agreed to leave carpeting and built-in shelving for a token amount, limiting the interruption of business. It was standard metal shelving but this was screened by new custom-built wooden shelves, locked cases from the old store, and the family's collection of antiques, including a Gustav Stickley table which had been a feature of Rosengren's since Chicago days. Although Rolly Hamilton was too ill to give it his flair, the new shop was well designed by Cam and Frank. It was well-lighted and spacious, with windows at the back overlooking one of the most pleasant parts of the River Walk. The Rosengrens later wondered why they thought they could make it where Waldenbooks had failed, but the store was charming and they would give it their best effort for five more years.

As she had since Florence's 1979 retirement, Cam handled all aspects of the business. She was ably assisted by Jeff Swartz and Nicki Prevou, née Beaudoin, who had both joined the staff before the move. Sue Shields continued to be the "storybook lady" and ran the children's department as she had since the Travis Park location. Paula Allen and others joined the staff comings and goings. One final children's story concerns Garland Buchanan, son of Bob Buchanan, one of Veltman's partners, and

One of the first parties at the store's location on Losoya Street was for Cam and Figgi's daughter, Emily. February 3, 1983.

Sally Buchanan [later president of the San Antonio Conservation Society, 1995-97]. The Buchanans owned the Kangaroo Court restaurant across the river from Rosengren's. As Garland recalled: "Because there was never anyone my age to play with when my parents took me to work with them, I would go over to the bookstore. They were very kind to me and let me sit behind the counter and read. I charged all the books to my dad who did not appreciate it when he got the bill."

Still, no matter how beloved the store was, Rosengren's would share the plight of independent bookstores nationwide in the 1980s, as Figgi explained:

> Times they were changing and the book business was, for sure. Television had already replaced the book as America's prime source for entertainment and information and the world of computers was right on its heels. Computer technology allowed nationwide distributors to emerge—notably Ingram in Nashville—and the weekly 'Ingram Order' quickly became a store necessity.
>
> Ironically, these new forces that would eventually be the undoing of bookstores as we had known them were, at first, a source of help. TV spread the word on individual titles to an extent nobody had dreamed of before. And when computers got going, they brought a revolution to the whole process of ordering books and getting them to the customer in a matter of days rather than weeks.

He concluded by observing that the same computer technology that allowed for the rise of national distributors also made national bookstore chains possible. By the time the store closed in 1987, all aspects of the book business had changed, including those which involved libraries. Rosengren's had continued to service several institutional library accounts, some of which had been established by Florence in the 1930s. The library systems at Fort Sam Houston and Trinity University were enlarged with Camille's involvement, but those relationships eventually fell prey to new technologies as well.

October 15, 1985, book party for Lyman Grant (left) and William A. Owens, editors of *The Letters of Roy Bedichek*. At right is Dave Cohen, long-time marketing manager for the University of Texas Press.

Noted Texana collector Al Lowman recorded his bittersweet memories of those final years:

> In mid-November, 1985, Rosengren's celebrated its 50th year in Texas with a publication party for Don Graham's *Texas: A Literary Portrait*, issued by the Corona Press of San Antonio. The store was crowded with customers and noted Texas writers who had come to celebrate. Here, together for the last time, were Florence and Rolly and Sue. Florence, shrunken and worn and too frail to hug, but looking stunning with her silver hair and bright red dress. The blue eyes had a bit of sparkle, and good humor still played across her broad features like occasional flashes of summer lightning. . . .[3]

On January 17, 1987, the San Antonio Historical Association chose Florence Rosengren as the recipient of its first Award of Merit, a recognition of her interest in the preservation and promotion of the history of San Antonio and South Texas. In a note to Ethel Moss, Frank Duane wrote: "Thought you'd like to see this evidence of a kind of victory. Mama was at the dinner for only half an hour but she made it. When Cam and I took her home, she had a glass of sherry and felt like someone who had scored a true and very personal touchdown."

Al Lowman also remembered the last autograph party he attended at Rosengren's on April 21, 1987:

> Larry McMurtry had just won the Pulitzer Prize for *Lonesome Dove*. To his everlasting credit, McMurtry would pass up other engagements in order to fill one at Rosengren's, although

he openly despises autograph parties . . . this one for his latest, *Texasville*. On this occasion, the store was mobbed. But for an enterprise that did not need any more disasters, it was frustrating that their stock of new books was soon exhausted because a fourth of their order had been mis-shipped to Corpus Christi. Even so, they sold an incredible 300-plus copies in two hours time.

One of the last book parties hosted by Rosengren's Books, on April 21, 1987. Larry McMurtry signs a copy of *Texasville* for Judy Burnside.

The store had announced it was for sale in May 1986 with an asking price of three hundred thousand dollars, to include the store's inventory of books and business equipment, but there were no takers. They were released from their lease, which had three and a half years left. Rosengren's was, after all, one of the last survivors. Even Joske's, which had been on Alamo Plaza for a century, had closed due to competition from national chain stores. [The business was founded as Joske Bros. Clothing and Dry Goods Merchants in 1889, when it was *the* place for cowboys to purchase work clothes.]

In mid-July 1987, Rosengren's customers received a mailed notice that after 52 years in Texas, the store would be closed. "All good things must end," the announcement concluded, "but not the memory and fellowship and pride." Comparing the situation to the Battle of the Alamo, "the invaders won and all the defenders died." Rosengren's succumbed to the fate of independent bookstores all across America.

Publishers Weekly prophesied the ominous epidemic and newspapers in every major city in America had to report similar deaths.

In her final days, Florence Kednay Rosengren found comfort in the Catholic faith of her childhood and died on August 19, 1988. Thus passed an unlikely hero, whom Ronnie Dugger once hailed as "the chief guardian of culture from here to Mexico City." Book critic Bryce Milligan's article celebrating her life in the *San Antonio Light* described her as "the ultimate bookwoman."

Florence and her beloved dog, Bippy, 1980.

11

Onward

Those who regarded the Rosengren family as a kind of intellectual nobility dreamed that there would be a continuity—that the mantle would pass to the next generation—assuming there would be a Rosengren's Books to inherit. Figgi and Cam's daughter, Emily, had worked in the store as a teenager and took pleasure in straightening out the shelves, but found the idea daunting:

> It was so quintessentially Grandmother's that it was unthinkable. She was better at it than I would ever be and had forgotten more about books than I could ever learn if I studied my whole life. But there was also the sense that you would not be allowed. . . . I can't imagine the peculiar kind of personality a granddaughter would require to have the patience and the lack of self to have been able to compete in that arena . . . the hubris to think that you could walk into those shoes. . . .
>
> Everybody adored Florence. She was everyone's mother, sister, best friend. She was able to play a variety of roles for the men and women who came into her life because she was accessible and available. She had not taken those parts of her and given them to another man after her husband died. Had there been, she could not have run the bookstore the way she did and given energy to others who gave energy back to her in a symbiotic relationship.

Hers was a life dedicated to reading. She came home to an empty house and sat up half the night reading. . . . Reading is what she did and she was so smart that she was able to get the gist of a book without having to read it in great detail. And she did not forget. She had that great love that kept the energy going. The study of literature was her life—the store was her life but the store also became her stage.[1]

By example, Florence encouraged Emily to make interesting choices and to follow her own dreams. But the bookstore would not be her stage.

Soon after HemisFair '68 closed, the film *Viva Max* (starring Peter Ustinov) was filmed in San Antonio. Frank Duane managed local casting for the film and Emily—then a student at Incarnate Word College—was hired as an "extra," one of a cast of thousands. It was then that she met Steve Ferry, who was property master for the film. Steve and Emily's friendship deepened through letters and two years later they married. At first, Emily served as Steve's assistant but later she went into business on her own. It was then necessary to convince the International Alliance of Theater and Stage Employees Local 44 that they ought to give her a union card in what had, heretofore, been an all-male purview. With the help of the National Labor Relations Board and a lawyer, Emily became the first female union card-carrying property master for the movie and television industry.

A property master must find and store every single prop which the actors will need when the actual shooting begins. Then when filming is underway, the property master is responsible for the continuity of the props—even the length of a lead pencil—as movies are seldom shot in temporal sequence. Among the scores of films on which Emily worked, some became cult classics like *The Right Stuff* (1983), *Raging Bull* (1996), and *Gattaca* (1997). One of her favorites, *Matilda* (1996), made a strong pro-literacy statement and reminded Emily of the *Madeline* books by Ludwig Bemelmans, beloved from her childhood.

In conclusion, a final observation from Emily:

When I first moved to California, the American Booksellers Association annual convention was in San Francisco. Grandma could not go, did not want to go, and suggested that I attend. Of course, the name tag said Rosengren. Everywhere I went, the publishers' reps and others would ask, "Are you Florence Rosengren's granddaughter? She is such a wonderful lady." It was reassuring because the person I thought she was was indeed who she was. She was respected and loved by readers across our great nation. For all the years that I can remember, there was a sense that she was "old school," that she was part of a dying breed that we were not going to see again. For this reason, the people at the ABA wanted to hold on to Grandma.

As did all whose minds and spirits were enriched for knowing Florence Rosengren.

Appendix 1

Florence's Legacy
in Texas Publishing

The following books were published by the University of Texas Press and the Texas A&M University Press under the direction of Frank Wardlaw, the founding director of both presses, with endowments generated by Florence Rosengren, and sometimes by her own suggestion. Many of these books debuted with author signings at Rosengren's Books. As can be seen, Florence's legacy continues to this day as three of the four series remain productive in 2014. The following lists are courtesy of Brian Contine, assistant editor of the University of Texas Press, and Gayla Christiansen of the Texas A&M University Press.

University of Texas Press:
The Elma Dill Russell Spencer
Foundation Series

Mary Motz Wills and Howard S. Irvin, *Roadside Flowers of Texas*, 1961

Rebecca Smith Lee, *Mary Austin Holley, a Biography*, 1962

Emily Edwards, *Painted Walls of Mexico from Prehistoric Times until Today*, 1966

Del Weniger, *Cacti of the Southwest: Texas, New Mexico, Oklahoma, Arkansas and Louisiana*, 1969

Jean Andrews, *Sea Shells of the Texas Coast*, 1971

Jean Andrews, *Shells and Shores of Texas*, 1977

Theodore Gentilz, *Gentilz: Artist of the Old Southwest*, 1974

Frederick Law Olmsted, *A Journey through Texas; or a Saddle-trip on the Southwestern Frontier*, 1978

Joseph D. McCutchan, *Mier Expedition Diary: A Texan Prisoner's Account*, 1978

Herman Seele, *The Cypress and Other Writings of a German Pioneer in Texas*, 1979

Alan Tennant and Michael Allender, *The Guadalupe Mountains of Texas*, 1980

Jean Andrews, *Texas Shells: A Field Guide*, 1981

David F. Prindle, *Petroleum Politics and the Texas Railroad Commission*, 1981

Terry Jordan, *Texas Graveyards: A Cultural Legacy*, 1982

Robert A. Vines, *Trees of North Texas*, 1982

University of Texas Press: The M. K. Brown Range Life Series

Cordia Sloan Duke and Joe B. Frantz, Six *Thousand Miles of Fence: Life on the XIT Ranch of Texas*, 1961

William Timmons, *Twilight on the Range: Recollections of a Latterday Cowboy*, 1962

Lester Fields Sheffy, *The Francklyn Land and Cattle Company: A Panhandle Enterprise, 1882-1957*, 1963

John Hendrix, *If I Can Do It Horseback: A Cow-Country Sketchbook*, 1964

Alva R. Stephens, *The Taft Ranch: A Texas Principality*, 1964

Dulcie Sullivan, *The LS Brand: The Story of a Texas Panhandle Ranch*, 1968

Virginia Taylor, *The Franco-Texas Land Company*, 1969

David B. Gracy, *Littlefield Lands: Colonization on the Texas Plains, 1912-1920*, 1968

B. R. (Billy Ray) Brunson, *The Texas Land and Development Company: A Panhandle Promotion, 1912-1956*, 1969

Sarah Ellen Roberts, *Alberta Homestead: Chronicle of a Pioneer Family*. Edited by Lathrop E. Roberts, 1971

Willie Newbury Lewis, *Tapadero: the Making of a Cowboy*, 1972

Frederick W. Rathjen, *The Texas Panhandle Frontier*, 1973

Sallie Reynolds Matthews; Drawings by E.M. Schiwetz, *Interwoven: A Pioneer Chronicle*, 1974

Erwin E. Smith and J. Evetts Haley, *Life on the Texas Range*, 1953, reissued 1973

David J. Murrah, *C.C. Slaughter: Rancher, Banker, Baptist*, 1981

Rufe LeFors, *Facts as I Remember Them: The Autobiography of Rufe LeFors* . Edited by John Allen Peterson, 1986

Jan Blodgett, *Land of Bright Promise: Advertising the Texas Panhandle and South Plains*, 1870- 1917, 1988

Dan Flores, *Caprock Canyonlands: Journeys into the Heart of the Southern Plains*, 1990

Lawrence Clayton, *Contemporary Ranches of Texas*, Photographs by Wyman Meinzer, 2001

Lawrence Clayton, Jim Hoy and Jerald Underwood, *Vaqueros, Cowboys and Buckaroos*, 2000

Bobby Bridger, *Buffalo Bill and Sitting Bull: Inventing the Wild West*, 2002

Robb Kendrick, *Still: Cowboys at the Start of the Twenty-First Century*, 2008

Rhondra Lashley Lopez, *Don't Make Me Go to Town: Ranchwomen of the Texas Hill Country*, 2011

Texas A&M University Press:
Louise Lindsey Merrick
Natural Environment Series

No. 1: *Texas Wildlife: Photographs from Texas Parks & Wildlife Magazine*, 1977

No. 2: Blair Pittman, *The Natural World of the Texas Big Thicket*, 1978

No. 3: Foreword by Frank T. Lively, Bob Parvin and Tommie Pinkard, *Landscapes of Texas: Photographs from Texas Highways Magazine*, 1980

No. 4: Jim Bones, *Texas West of the Pecos*, 1981

No. 5: John L. Tveten, *Coastal Texas: Water, Land, and Wildlife*, 1982

No. 6: Ilo Hiller, *Young Naturalists: From Texas Parks and Wildlife Magazine*, 1983

No. 7: Jack Pearl Lewis, *Texas in Bloom: Photographs from Texas Highways Magazine*, 1984

No. 8: *Wild Flowers Portfolio*, 1985

No. 9: Ilo Hiller, *Introducing Birds to Young Naturalists: From Texas Parks & Wildlife Magazine*, 1989

No. 10: Ilo Hiller, *Introducing Mammals to Young Naturalists: From Texas Parks & Wildlife Magazine*, 1990.

No. 11: Howard Peacock, ed., *The Nature of Texas: A Feast of Native Beauty from Texas Highways Magazine*, 1990

No. 12: Roland H. Wauer , *Birder's Mexico*, 1992

No. 13: Thomas J. Lyon and Peter Stine, eds., *On Nature's Terms: Contemporary Voices*, 1992

No. 14: *Favorite Texas Birds* (Boxed cassette tape), 1993

No. 15: Frederick R. Gehlbach, *Mountain Islands and Desert Seas: A Natural History of the U.S.–Mexican Borderlands*, 1981

No. 16: Elizabeth C. Mundall, William J. Sheffield and Charles W. Ramsey, *Exotics on the Range: The Texas Example*, 1994

No. 17: David Bruce, *Bird of Jove*, 1994

No. 18: Robert Benson and Karen Benson, *Sounds of Texas Birds* (cassette tape and CD), 1994

No. 19: Alwyn Scarth, *Volcanoes: An Introduction*, 1994

No. 20: Marcia Myers Bonta , ed., *American Women Afield: Writings by Pioneering Women Naturalists*, 1995

No. 21: James Symons, *Drinking Water: Refreshing Answers to All Your Questions*, 1995

No. 22: Louis Jacobs; Illustrations by Karen Carr, *Lone Star Dinosaurs*, 1995

No. 23: Alexander F. Skutch, *The Minds of Birds*, 1996

No. 24: Elizabeth Silverthorne, *Legends and Lore of Texas Wildflowers*, 1996

No. 25: Ilo Hiller, *The White-Tailed Deer*, 1996

No. 26: Donald Finley, *Mad Dogs: The New Rabies Plague*, 1998

No. 27: Joseph James Shomon, *Wild Edens: Africa's Premier Game Parks and Their Wildlife*, 1998

No. 28: D. Gentry Steele, *Land of the Desert Sun: Texas' Big Bend Country*, 1998

No. 29: Alexander F. Skutch; Illustrations by Dana Gardner, *Trogons, Laughing Falcons, and Other Neotropical Birds*, 1999

No. 30: Roland H. Wauer; Illustrations by Ralph Scott, Heralds of Spring in Texas, 1999

No. 31: Blair Pittman, *Texas Caves*, 1999

No. 32: Verne Huser, *Rivers of Texas*, 2004 (delayed pub.)

No. 33: Roland H. Wauer and Carl M. Fleming, *Naturalist's Big Bend: An Introduction to the Trees and Shrubs, Wildflowers, Cacti, Mammals, Birds, Reptiles and Amphibians, Fish, and Insects*, 2001

No. 34: Paul Freed, O*f Golden Toads and Serpents' Roads*, 2003

No. 35: Mark T. Adams, *Chasing Birds across Texas: A Birding Big Year*, 2003

No. 36: Mark W. Lockwood and Brush Freeman, *The TOS Handbook of Texas Birds*, 2004

No. 37: Paul D. Kyle and Georgean Z. Kyle, *Chimney Swifts: America's Mysterious Birds above the Fireplace*, 2005

No. 38: Paul D. Kyle, *Chimney Swift Towers: New Habitat for America's Mysterious Birds*, 2005

No. 39: Jan Wrede, *Trees, Shrubs, and Vines of the Texas Hill Country: A Field Guide,* 2005

No. 40: Brian Loflin and Shirley Loflin, *Grasses of the Texas Hill Country: A Field Guide*, 2006

No. 41: Jeffrey Greene; Illustrations by Margaret Bamberger. *Water from Stone: The Story of Selah, Bamberger Ranch Preserve*, 2007

No. 42: Greg W. Lasley, *Greg Lasley's Texas Wildlife Portraits*, 2008

No. 43: Dorothy Chapman Saunders; edited by Henry M. Reeves and Roy E. Tomlinson, *Chico, George, the Birds, and Me: The Mexican Travelogue of a Woman Naturalist, 1948-1949*, 2008

No. 44: Jim Stanley, *Hill Country Landowner's Guide*, 2009

No. 45: Cheryl Hazeltine, *Cheryl Hazeltine's Central Texas Gardener*, 2010

No. 46: Geyata Ajilvsgi, *Butterfly Gardening for Texas,* 2013

No. 47: Mark W. Lockwood and Brush Freeman, *The TOS Handbook of Texas Birds,* Second Edition, 2014

Texas A&M University Press: Elma Dill Russell Spencer Series

No. 1: Joe B. Frantz, *Aspects of the American West*, 1976

No. 2: Howard R. Lamar, *The Trader on the American Frontier: Myth's Victim*, 1977

No. 3: Ray A. Billington, *America's Frontier Culture*, 1977

No. 4: Dan Kilgore, *How Did Davy Die?*, 1982

No. 5: C. L. Sonnichsen, *Grave of John W. Hardin*, 1979

No. 6: Margaret Swett Henson, *Juan Davis Bradburn: A Reappraisal of the Mexican Commander of Anahuac*, 1982

No. 7: L. D. Clark, *Civil War Recollections of James Lemuel Clark*, 1984

No. 8: Donald E. Worcester, *The Texas Longhorn: Relic of the Past, Asset for the Future*, 1987

No. 9: Muriel Marshall, *Red Hole in Time,* 1988

No. 10: A. B. Clarke, *Travels in Mexico and California*, 1989

No. 11: Robert Ryal Miller, *Mexican War Journal and Letters of Ralph K. Kirkham*, 1991

No. 12: Glen E. Lich, *Regional Studies: The Interplay of Land and People*, 1992

No. 13: Frederick Zeh, *An Immigrant Soldier in the Mexican War*, 1995

No. 14: Muriel Marshall, *Where Rivers Meet: Lore from the Colorado Frontier*, 1996

No. 15: Marc Simmons, *Massacre on the Lordsburg Road: A Tragedy of the Apache Wars*, 1997

No. 16: Robert S. Ove and H. Henrietta Stockel, *Geronimo's Kids: A Teacher's Lessons on the Apache Reservation*, 1997

No. 17: Wallace Ohrt, *Defiant Peacemaker: Nicholas Trist in the Mexican War,* 1997

No. 18: David La Vere, *Life among the Texas Indians: The WPA Narratives*, 1998

No. 19: Paul H. Carlson, *The Plains Indians,* 1998

No. 20: Kelly F. Himmel, *The Conquest of the Karankawas and the Tonkawas, 1821-1859,* 1999

No. 21: H. Henrietta Stockel, *Chiricahua Apache Women and Children: Safekeepers of the Heritage*, 2000

No. 22: Jorge Iber, *Hispanics in the Mormon Zion, 1912-1999*, 2000

No. 23: Gerald Betty, *Comanche Society: Before the Reservation*, 2002

No. 24: Adrienne Caughfield, *True Women and Westward Expansion,* 2002

No. 25: Anne H. Sutherland, *The Robertsons, the Sutherlands, and the Making of Texas*, 2006

No. 26: Jovita González, edited by María Eugenia Cotera, *Life Along the Border: A Landmark Tejana Thesis*, 2006

No. 27: Gregg Cantrell and Elizabeth H. Turner, eds., *Lone Star Pasts: Memory and History in Texas*, 2007

No. 28: Stuart Reid, *The Secret War for Texas*, 2007

No. 29: H. Sophie Burton and F. Todd Smith, *Colonial Natchitoches: A Creole Community on the Louisiana-Texas Frontier*, 2008

No. 30: Kyle G. Wilkison, *Yeomen, Sharecroppers, and Socialists: Plain Folk Protest in Texas, 1870-1914*, 2008

No. 31: Jimmy L. Bryan Jr., *More Zeal Than Discretion: The Westward Adventures of Walter P. Lane*, 2008

No. 32: S. R. Martin, *On the Move: A Black Family's Western Saga*, 2009

No. 33: Margaret S. Henson, and edited by Donald E. Willett, *The Texas That Might Have Been: Sam Houston's Foes Write to Albert Sidney Johnston*, 2009

No. 34: Jesús F. de la Teja, *Tejano Leadership in Mexican and Revolutionary Texas*, 2010

No. 35: David O'Donald Cullen and Kyle G. Wilkison, eds., *The Texas Left: The Radical Roots of Lone Star Liberalism*, 2010

No. 36: Dan Kilgore and James E. Crisp, *How Did Davy Die? And Why Do We Care So Much?* Commemorative Edition, 2010

No. 37: H. Henrietta Stockel, *Drumbeats from Mescalero: Conversations with Apache Elders, Warriors, and Horseholders*, 2011

No. 38: William S. Kiser, *Turmoil on the Rio Grande: History of the Mesilla Valley, 1846-1865*, 2011

No. 39: David O'Donald Cullen and Kyle G. Wilkison, eds., *The Texas Right: The Radical Roots of Lone Star Conservatism*, 2014

Appendix 2

Concerning
the Rosengren Papers

After Rosengren's Books closed its final location on Losoya Street above the River Walk in 1987, random collections of materials—business records, several generations of family correspondence, photographs, manuscripts, and works-in-progress—were packed in over a hundred file boxes and deposited in several storage facilities. An index of the contents of these boxes was begun in 1986 (boxes 01- 80) with another listing begun in 1995 (boxes 1-37 A). Box 42—containing Florence Rosengren's personal correspondence, which she kept near-at-hand—remains with the family.

The Alamo Research Center, formerly the Daughters of the Republic of Texas (DRT) Library, holds a collection donated by the Rosengren family related to the River Road Country Day School, as well as a large number of books donated to the library by Florence over the course of fifty years.

The Rosengren family donated seventeen boxes of materials related specifically to their various bookstores to the Wittliff Collections, Alkek Library, Texas State University-San Marcos—a decision based on their long friendship with William Wittliff. The first accession of materials was made in 2010 with three subsequent donations in 2011. All of these materials have been rehoused in acid-free folders and boxes and basic preservation work has been completed. A detailed listing of the contents has also been created, according to Katharine A. Salzmann, lead archivist. At present, the balance of the collection is housed at a private location.

Further evidence of the relationship between Wittliff and the Rosengrens surfaced after the bookstore closing. Wittliff established the Encino Press (its first imprint in 1965) and produced limited editions distinguished by excellence of design and quality of content. Early on, as an encouragement to the press, Florence placed a standing order for ten or more copies of everything Encino printed. When the store closed, wrapped packages of unsold books were discovered—never "remaindered" as is the usual business custom.

Appendix 3
Frank Duane Rosengren
1926 – 2010

Frank Duane Rosengren was a playwright, poet, lyricist, screenwriter and producer. He started early. He was only ten years old when his first play, "The Nuts at the Roundtable," was published in *Story Parade: A Magazine for Boys and Girls.* He graduated from Jefferson High School in 1944 and almost immediately enlisted in the U.S. Army Air Forces. He served in Special Services from 1944 to 1946. He spent the next two years working in the editorial department at Churusbusco Studios in Mexico City, then attended the University of Chicago, graduating in 1951.

Frank married Emily Camille Sweeney on January 13, 1951. Frank's play, "Walls Rise Up," was produced that year by Margo Jones at Theatre 51 in Dallas. Frank became a staff writer on the CBS television series, "Omnibus." Some of his plays and screenplays written at this time include: "Suddenly, A Thief"(1952), "Faces for Charlie" (1954), "A Delicate Question" (1956), "Touch Fire" (1957), "Jimmy and The River" (1958), "Guitar" (1959), "A Smaller Joy" (1960), and "Teeth of the Devil" (1961). After returning to San Antonio, his plays "San Jose Story" (1962) and "Prophets of Light" (1966) were produced locally.

Frank was the editor of HemisFair '68's newsletter, *El Abrazo,* and Special Consultant on Theme

Development. After HemisFair, he helped get public television station KLRN off the ground, serving as an executive producer there for ten years. In 1974 he received a grant from the National Endowment for the Humanities to narrate, write and produce "Pilgrims to the West," depicting Spanish colonization in the Southwest. Frank was simply a "jack-of-all-genres" when it came to theatrical, television, and film writing and production.

His obituary in the *San Antonio Express-News* concluded thus: "A wellspring of area historical lore, connoisseur of story-telling, possessor of a writer's observational skills, gifted conversationalist and blessed with ample wit, charm, curiosity and a diplomat's temperament, Frank Rosengren was the rare 'scholar and a gentleman' who truly lived up to the justly earned appellation." Indeed.

Notes

Chapter 1

1. Interview by Mary Carolyn Hollers George (hereafter MCHG) with Frank Duane and Camille Rosengren, July 2, 1996.

To differentiate between the father, Frank Rosengren Sr. and his son, the son will be cited as Frank Duane, the name he used as author or as "Figgi," his nickname.

2. Concerning Frank Rosengren's career as a musician, letter from Frank Duane to MCHG, November 5, 2008.

3. After Frank Rosengren's death, his sheet music collection was donated to the San Antonio Public Library but was subsequently "misplaced." Letter from Frank Duane to MCHG, May 26, 2008.

4. Interview by MCHG with Frank Duane, January 16, 1997.

5. For additional information about the Chicago Literary Renaissance as well as the collapse of law and order during the Prohibition years, see the Electronic Encyclopedia of Chicago @ 2005, Chicago Historical Society, The Encyclopedia of Chicago @ 2004 The Newbery Library.

6. Frank's 1920 dollars would translate to 2014 dollars at a rate of 1 : 12.5—so his $250 quick profit would be equivalent to about $3,125 today.

7. The Tree Studio Building, Annexes and Courtyard were built in 1894 – 1913.

Designed to serve as artists' studios, a legal trust stipulated that only artists could live in the Tree Studios. It may be surmised that a business named Rosengren's Book and Art Galleries was deemed acceptable as a tenant, although the "art gallery" may have been in name only. The State Street Building was listed as a Chicago Landmark in 1997 amid concern that the complex would be demolished to make way for a high rise tower. In 2001, the restoration of the property began and the

Annexes and Courtyard were added to the listing. The complex was also placed on the National Register of Historic Places in 1974. City of Chicago: Chicago Landmarks. Site visit by MCH and W. Eugene George in June 2004.

8. Ill health prevented Frank Rosengren Sr. from completing work-in-progress on his bibliography. A similar work titled *U.S.-IANA,* compiled by Wright Howes, would be published by R.R. Bowker Company for the Newbery Library in 1954 and re-published in 1962. Howes died at 95 in 1978. Letter, FDR to MCHG, February 28, 2009.

9. *Fred Allen's Letters* was published by Doubleday in 1965. A large box of Allen-Rosengren correspondence, which was discovered in the Rosengren family papers, was entrusted to the author. After the death of Frank Duane Rosengren in May, 2010, and with the family's authorization, these materials were transferred to the Southwestern Writers Collection, Wittliff Collections.

Also an item in the "Around the Plaza" column by Renwicke Cary in the *San Antonio Light*, April 8, 1965, p. 22.

Chapter 2

1. Interview, Frank Duane and Camille Rosengren, July 2, 1996.

2. In 1965, when she was 80 years old, Blanche Kednay donated her entire collection of 235 books and other documents to the Lake County Library System.

The Hammond Times, October 17, 1965, p.7. Robert Andrews also wrote an article titled "She Knows the Arctic but Stays Home" October 8, 1931 in the *Chicago Daily News*.

3. Frank Rosengren's first wife was licensed as an attorney about 1919 and was probably somewhat his senior. The second was a brief marriage to a show business personage. Relevant divorce papers and letters are known to exist but have not been rediscovered in the Rosengren family papers. It is reasonable to assume that these marriages occurred after World War I and before the first bookstore was opened.

4. FDR to MCHG, July 2, 1996.

Chapter 3

1. David Anton Randall, *The J. K. Lilly Collection of Edgar Allan Poe: An Account of Its Formation* (Indiana University Press, 1964) pp. 10-15. Randall quotes Harry Hansen's column on pp. 14-15. David Randall was manager of the rare book department at Charles Scribner's Sons in New York before becoming the first director of the Lilly Library. Considered a "legendary bookman," he worked closely with Eli Lilly to shape the remarkable rare book collections at Indiana University, Bloomington.

2. The Hertzberg Circus Collection and Museum was established by Harry Hertzberg which he bequeathed to the San Antonio Public Library. It is the oldest public circus collection in the United States. For many years, it housed the rare books collection of the San Antonio Public Library, a poor arrangement since windows opened directly onto the river.

Chapter 4

1. Norman Sherry, *The Life of Graham Greene: 1904-1939* (New York: Penguin Books, 1989) 1: 665-668. Also personal communication, Norman Sherry to MCHG regarding research for her history of the Anglo-Texan Society which was founded by Greene in 1953. Dr. Sherry is on the faculty of Trinity University in San Antonio.

2. George Sessions Perry. *Texas: A World in Itself* (New York: Whittlesey House / McGraw Hill, 1942) pp. x-xi.

3. The Sibyl Browne Papers 1912-1979 with biographical notes including information about her mother, Miss Hetty, were deposited in the Daughters of the Republic of Texas Library at the Alamo by the executor of her estate, Leslie Fenstermaker.

In addition, the Frank Duane Rosengren collection at the DRT Library includes materials about the River Road Country Day School: seventeen photographs from the mid 1920s as well as clippings and documents, for example, a publication for the 1928-1929 school session; an article titled "A Country School in the City" in the July 11, 1926 edition of the *San Antonio*

Express; and Bonnie Sue Jacobs' article in the July 1, 1976 issue of the *North San Antonio Times* titled "River Road School Stressed Natural Surroundings."

Sibyl Browne lived upstairs in the building constructed for the River Road Country Day School from 1958 until her death in 1979. Miss Hetty lived with her daughter until her death in 1966.

The author, MCHG, and her family lived on the first floor of the school building from 1954 to 1958. From 1978 to 1995, she lived at 112 Anastacia in what had been a barn moved from a site nearby to serve as an art studio for the school—outside the gate to the Zambrano house. In that second period, architect Morgan Price lived in the cottage in the back yard referred to as "the Jacalita," followed by Kenneth Wolfson, principal bassoonist with the San Antonio Symphony. Jim Cullum of Happy Jazz Band fame has owned and lived in various properties in the Anastacia compound.

4. See entries for José Dario Zambrano and Juan José Manuel Vicente Zambrano, two of Mario's sons, in the *New Handbook of Texas*. Regarding the Zambrano house—if only those ancient walls could tell what they witnessed in the 1800s.

5. A City of San Antonio historic structures monument was erected alongside the acequia route on March 25, 2012.

6. Notes accompanying photographs in the Rosengren Collection in the DRT Library are the source for information about the school house building.

7. Frank Lloyd Wright's childhood instruction by the Froebel System of Education using construction with blocks contributed significantly to his development as an architect.

8. A listing of his literary accomplishments accompanied the announcement by Porter Loring of the memorial service following his death on April 29, 2010.

9. An oral history with Frank and Camille Rosengren conducted by Bill Sibley of the Neighborhood History Committee, River Road Neighborhood Association, on August 20, 2008. The extent of Our Lady of Sorrows parish was diminished when the route of the North Expressway connecting downtown with its northern suburbs was constructed in the

mid-1970s—in spite of fierce opposition. Through the years, a priest from the church would occasionally appear at the gate accessing the Zambrano-Rosengren property and be turned away—until the last year of Florence's life, when he would be welcomed as a comforting presence.

10. The Tuesday Musical Club, founded by Anna Goodman Hertzberg in 1901, met nearby at 521 W. Euclid Ave. The present location on North St. Mary's Street inside Brackenridge Park was not built until 1950. Mrs. Hertzberg was the force behind the construction of the adjacent Sunken Garden Theater, which opened in July, 1930.

11. During World War II while serving in England [1943-44], Eugene George spent his off-duty hours on the fifth floor of Foyles where the architecture books were located.

Alfred Bossom, president of the Anglo-Texan Society from the mid-1950s until his death in 1965, had an immensely successful architecture practice in the United States. He specialized during the early 1920s in the design of skyscrapers. With the conviction that skyscrapers were unsuitable for the British Isles, he forsook architecture upon his return to the UK in 1926 and began a new life in public service.

12. The Milam Building was designated a National Mechanical Engineering Heritage Site in a ceremony on August 23, 1991. To quote from the commemorative brochure: "When it opened in January 1928, San Antonio's 21-story Milam Building, originally owned by the Travis Investment Company, was the nation's tallest brick and reinforced-concrete structure—taller than comparable concrete-framed buildings in New York and Chicago—and the first high-rise air-conditioned office building in the country."

The Milam Building was the fourth site to be so designated by the American Society of Mechanical Engineers. The third in the trio of skyscrapers, the Smith-Young Tower, was purchased by H.B. Zachry in 1940 but was not centrally air-conditioned until 1957. Research including documentation of the Milam Building was made available to the author by Martha Doty Freeman.

13. Frank Duane and Camille Rosengren interview, February 5, 1997.

14. Letter, Frank Duane to MCHG, November 30, 2008. The changing—then vanishing—role of the publisher's rep and the reasons for its demise are fully described in this letter as well as their importance in the history of the store, well into the 1970s.

15. Frank Duane and Camille Rosengren interview, July 2, 1996.

16. A back room of the shop—furnished like a living room—also housed the rare book collection and was a gathering place for small groups. It became a meeting place for San Antonio's intellectuals, authors (and would-be-ones), and for people who simply liked to talk about books. A frequent visitor, Green Peyton Wertenbaker, author of *San Antonio: City in the Sun*, wrote: "It was a lovely intellectual oasis for people for whom conversation is like cool water bubbling from a spring." [Quoted from the *San Antonio Light*, April 18, 1982, 3-c.]

The author and her husband, Eugene George, interviewed Edward Maggs in London on May 20, 1997. The fifth generation of bookselling Maggses, Edward was first associated with the family business in 1979-80. Prior to that, he worked for a brief period for publisher and bookseller John Jenkins of Austin, Texas —to "learn the business." Edward is the grandson of Frank Maggs with whom Frank Rosengren dealt in 1939.

The San Antonio Public Library purchased the King James Bible (1611) from Rosengren's in 1945 with funds from a bequest by Harry Hertzberg. It was stored in a vault for 66 years until July of 2011 when it was put on display for the first time since its acquisition. "King James Bible from 1611 on display in San Antonio" by Scott Huddleston, *San Antonio Express-News*, reprinted in the *Austin American Statesman*, July 2011.

17. Frank and Camille Rosengren, interview, July 2, 1996

18. Uriah Maggs—founder of the business—set up a market street stall in the 1850s near Paddington Station, London. By the 1880s, it had evolved into a Victorian bookstore. The antiquarian book trade burgeoned due to (1) the impoverishment of the aristocracy and (2) the prosperity of American tycoons who were eager to acquire impressive

libraries. This continued through the climactic period leading up to World War II. Today, Maggs Bros. Ltd. holds a Royal Warrant: By appointment to Her Majesty The Queen, Purveyors of Rare Books & Manuscripts."

As a curious note, the connection between Maggs Bros. and Rosengren's brought another Chicago-born bookman to San Antonio decades later. David Bowen, a New York-based actor and producer, was also the author of several books on Latin America and one on race relations. Along the way, he had studied rare book bibliography at Maggs in the 1950s. When he was offered a job consulting for the 1968 HemisFair in San Antonio, he jumped at the chance to come to what had been described to him as "one of the loveliest spots on earth with one of the best of all bookstores." Bowen owned two rare book stores in San Antonio, Village Books and On Paper, and he founded Corona Publishing Company. Among other things, he hired a young cataloger, Bryce Milligan, and published his first two books. Milligan's first book signing—which he was honored to share with future poet laureate of Texas, Rosemary Catacalos, was held at Rosengren's in 1984. Milligan, who was himself an employee of Rosengren's 1980-1981, has been the publisher of Wings Press since 1995.

19. Personal communication from R.L. (Robert) Dewar to MCHG, February 13, 1999 who remembered that if his father was not in his office or traveling, you could probably find him at Rosengren's.

20. Interview, Al Lowman by MCHG, October 1, 1997.

21. Books signed by authors from the Rosengrens' book signing events were donated to the J.E. and L.E. Mabee Library of the University of the Incarnate Word and are shelved together in the Special Collections Room, according to Mary Jinks, Librarian.

22. Paula Allen described Frost's visit in her "A Look Back" column in the *San Antonio Express News*. Allen worked at Rosengren's in the final years. Also, interview, Frank and Camille Rosengren, October 10, 1997. The Frosts stayed in a small, two-gabled bungalow, "half-timbered," with a cobblestone chimney, numbered then and now 113.

Chapter 5

1. Interviews with Frank Duane and Camille Rosengren, cited in previous chapters, are the sources for Chapter Five. Additional points of reference will be noted.

2. Interview by MCHG with Emily Rosengren Ferry, Frank Duane and Cam Rosengren's daughter, Florence's granddaughter, August 8, 1996.

3. Interview by MCHG with Ethel Marie Moss, January 7, 1997, in Garland, Texas.

4. Interview by MCHG with Dorothy Steinbomer Kendall, February 15, 1995.

5. Mary Carolyn Hollers George, *Mary Bonner: Impressions of a Printmaker* (San Antonio: Trinity University Press, 1982), pp. 41-42.

6. The annual report also included a list of board members during this ten year period. Attempting to economize in every way, no regular annual library reports were printed after the 1929-30 fiscal year.

7. Following his death in 1940, Harry Hertzberg's personal collection of more than 20,000 volumes was bequeathed to the San Antonio Public Library including major holdings in circus memorabilia. Also see Chapter Four, note 2.

8. When the Rosengrens opened their shop in the Milam Building, there was an active bookstore in the department store, Wolff and Marx, nearby on West Houston Street at Soledad and, soon thereafter, another on Alamo Plaza in Joske's of Texas. *Worley's San Antonio City Directory*, 1936-37, listed Rosengren's and fifteen other bookstores around town, including four which specialized in Spanish language publications—and Brock's, the legendary second-hand bookstore which would still be in business decades later.

The city actually had a long history of bookstores. The oldest by far was Nic Tengg's Bookstore, which operated from 1854 to the mid-20th century, most of that time at 220 E. Commerce. Started by Julius Berends. Tengg worked in the store as a boy and bought the store in 1874 when Berends returned to Switzerland. Tengg had four sons, all of whom worked in the store for most of their lives. A Mr. E. E.

Cervantes worked there for 74 years, until he was 92. The store shut down when the Groos National Bank bought the land and turned it into a parking lot.

Two other stores were active in the late 19th century: Henry A. Moos Books, 618 E. Commerce, 1890s to 1920s. Sidney P. Gamble's Bookstore on West Commerce. Active from the 1860s to 1890s.

9. At Fort Sam Houston—in addition to the main library—there were small branch libraries scattered around the post. These were air-conditioned which the wooden barracks were not, even as late as the 1960s. In a letter from Morgan Price to MCHG dated July 24, 2011, he wrote about his six months on active duty with the Army Reserve in 1963: "I will always be grateful to the army program which provided these small libraries which offered a refuge from the heat and loneliness in off-duty hours."

10. Interview by MCHG with Joselyn Levi, April 14, 1995, who had a family relationship with the Lippincott publishing house.

11. See note 2, Emily Rosengren Ferry.

12. Letter from John Douglas to MCHG, undated. John and Frannie Douglas have owned the Twig Book Shop for over a decade. It recently moved to the Pearl Brewery redevelopment. Douglas also owns the interfaith bookstore, Viva, on Broadway.

13. See note 2, Emily Rosengren Ferry.

Chapter 6

1. The information in Chapter Six was drawn from the following sources including interviews with Frank Duane and Camille Rosengren previously cited: Letter, Frank Duane Rosengren to MCHG describing events in the 1940s; "Memories of the Rosengrens During World War II" by Lola Curbo Attanasio, written in response to an inquiry by MCHG, April 3, 1998; Ethel Marie Moss interview January 7, 1997; Kent Kennan interview April 4, 1995; Amy Freeman Lee interview October 28, 1994; correspondence between MCHG and Dr. Gerald Taylor in the month of

February 1997; and telephone interview with Daniel Schorr by MCHG April 12, 1995, followed by a reunion with Schorr and the Rosengrens at 104 Anastacia on November 4, 1997. Also present—Amy Freeman Lee, W. Eugene George and MCHG. Schorr was in town to present a lecture at UT-San Antonio titled "Forgive Us Our Press Passes." Other than a brief stop over a decade earlier, this was the journalist's first return to San Antonio since his days at Fort Sam Houston—which he mentions in *Staying Tuned: A Life in Journalism* (New York: Pocket Books, 2001).

Chapter 7

1. The information in Chapter Seven was drawn from the previously cited interviews with Frank Duane and Camille Rosengren and Emily Rosengren Ferry.

2. In 1952, Walter Loughridge became Judge of the 37th District Court. Phone interview by the author with Ann Loughridge McClanahan, February 19, 1997.

3. In the 1950s, familiar street patterns and their names changed when a system of expressways encircled San Antonio's urban core. Some maps of the period incorrectly swapped the names of Travis and Pecan Streets, but this was never the case on the ground.

4. For more about this issue, see Mary Carolyn Hollers George, *O'Neil Ford, Architect*, (College Station: Texas A&M University Press, 1992), p. 124. Also a similar threat to the city's only other downtown park, Main Plaza, which dates from the Spanish Colonial period. Both occurred during Wanda Graham Ford's first year as president of the San Antonio Conservation Society.

5. Interview by MCHG with Robert Lynn Batts Tobin, January 30, 1995.

At age 20, Tobin served as president of the Children's Service Bureau and, several years later, he became chairman of the Board of Managers of the Bexar County Hospital district—a reflection of his concern for indigent children and the health needs of the poor. In the decades to come, he was also a major benefactor of the Metropolitan Opera and the Museum of Modern Art in New York City, the Santa Fe Opera and the Spoleto Festival of Two Worlds in Italy. But his involvement with the Marion Koogler McNay Art Museum which commenced with his meeting John Leeper in 1950 would remain his life-long passion. "Prominent Arts Patron Tobin Dies," *San Antonio Express-News*, April 27, 2000.

6. Lyle Williams, Curator of Prints and Drawings, McNay Art Museum, communication on July 30, 2012.

7. Interview by MCHG with John Palmer Leeper, March 13, 1995.

In order not to be in competition with Florence, there would not be a bookstore in the museum until Rosengren's closed in 1987.

8. In 1980, for example, the *Today Show* did a morning story on a new book published by Abbeville Press, a huge (over four feet tall) leather-bound tome, *The Vatican Frescoes of Michelangelo*, with an equally huge price tag of $9,000. The clerk at the time, Bryce Milligan, suggested that Cam try to sell a copy to Robert Tobin. Cam called and Tobin bought it immediately.

9. Lyle Williams provided the author with copies of the McNay Annual Reports for 1968 and 1971.

10. The Rosengren-Dobie letter dated February 3, 1958 is deposited in the Harry Ransom Humanities Research Center of the University of Texas at Austin.

11. For a full account of Frank Duane's accomplishments in theater and television production, see his obituary on May 5, 2010, Porter Loring.

Chapter 8

1. The Wardlaw-Rosengren letter of February 14, 1977 was sent to the author by Gayla Christiansen of the Texas A&M University Press. She was the first person hired by Frank Wardlaw when he arrived in College Station in 1974. Any other correspondence they had was lost in February 1979 when a fire destroyed the building which housed the press.

2. "Changing Times: The Life and Death of a Bookstore" by Al Lowman, published in *AB Bookman's Weekly*, March 14,

1988, p. 1071, is the source for Florence Rosengren's role in the endowment of the M.K. Brown Series.

For more about British-owned ranching interests in Texas, see Thomas W. Cutrer's *The English in Texas*, published by the University of Texas Institute of Texan Cultures at San Antonio, 1985.

The 25,610-square-mile Panhandle of Texas comprises the northernmost twenty-six counties of the state.

3. Henry C. Dethloff, *A Bookmark: Texas A&M University Press* (College Station: Texas A&M University Press, 1999), 7-13.

Three Men in Texas: Essays by Their Friends in the Texas Observer, edited by Ronnie Dugger and published in 1967 by the University of Texas Press, is a tribute to "an incomparable triumvirate"—Webb, Dobie, and Bedicek—historian, folklorist, and naturalist.

4. They may well have come to regret their decision. *The Poky Little Puppy* by Lowrey and illustrated by Gustaf Tenggren was first published in 1942 and is still in print. In 2007, a 65th anniversary edition of what has become one of the bestselling picture books of all time was published by Little Golden Books.

5. MCHG interview with John Igo, January 11, 1995.

6.. John Igo has published twelve books on poetry including *The Third Temptation of St. John* (National Society of Arts and Letters award), *God of Gardens* (Southwest Writers Conference Publication Award) and *Alien* (Poetry Society Foundation). In addition, he has authored books of prose and several plays. In 1985, his script for "Our Children: The Next Generation" received an Emmy. He has served as volunteer project manager of the Theater Archive for the Friends of the San Antonio Public Library.

Chapter 9

1. Interview by MCHG with Amy Freeman Lee, October 28, 1994.

2. Ed Harte's father, Houston Harte, founder of the Harte-Hanks newspaper empire, authored a book of Old Testament stories titled *In Our Image*. Although it was

published in 1949 by the Oxford University Press, then one of Rosengren's top suppliers, no evidence can be found of a book signing party at the shop in the Milam building. That Frank Rosengren died that same year may explain the omission.

3. Letter from Maury Maverick Jr. to MCHG, March 22, 1995. His relationship to the Rosengrens dated back to his days at the River Road Country Day School. He was a liberal and defender of civil liberties as was his father who was mayor of San Antonio in 1939-1941 and an early customer of the bookstore.

4. Frank Duane was the author of the entry on HemisFair '68 in the *New Handbook of Texas.* For additional information, see *O'Neil Ford: Architect* by MCHG, pp. 182-196.

5. MCHG interview with Phillip and Linda Hardberger, February 7, 1995.

Phil (Phillip) Hardberger served as executive secretary of the Peace Corps during the administration of President John F. Kennedy (1961–1963). Under President Lyndon B. Johnson (1963–1969), he was special assistant to the director of the U.S. Office of Economic Opportunity. In the 1990s in San Antonio, he was appointed Chief Justice of the Fourth Court of Appeals. Hardberger served two terms as Mayor of San Antonio, from 2005 to 2009. He was known not only for his efforts at both preservation and revitalization of the central city, but as a strong advocate for arts funding and the promotion of regional culture.

The designation of Main Plaza as one of the ten "Great Public Places in the US" was made by the American Planning Association.

Chapter 10

1. The primary source for Chapter Ten are interviews with Frank and Camille Rosengren cited in notes for previous chapters. The Higgins Book Shop was purchased from Dr. H. R. Higgins by Robert Jornayvaz in 1977, who sold it to Harris Smithson in 1980. Unable to sell the store to the Rosengrens, he combined it with an existing store, The Twig Book Shop, which is now San Antonio's only remaining independent book

store, recently re-located to the development in the old Pearl Brewery at the northern end of the river extension.

2. While the exact date and page number for Jan Jarboe's article are missing, it must have been soon after April 1, 1982 in the *San Antonio Express-News*.

3. Al Lowman, "Changing Times," *AB Bookman's Weekly*, March 14, 1988, 1073-74, is the source for high points in the last years before Rosengren's closed.

In 2005, Al Lowman and his wife, Darlyne, donated an archive of J. Frank Dobie's published materials to the Wittliff Collections, Southwestern Writers Collection, at Texas State University in San Marcos.

Chapter 11

1. Interview by the author with Emily Rosengren Ferry, August 8, 1996. Also "Prop Master Carries Card, Check," by Suzanne Diehl, *North San Antonio Times*, April 16, 1981, p.2.

Sources Consulted

The author's research materials listed below are deposited in the University of Texas at San Antonio Library Special Collections with the Mary Carolyn Hollers George Papers.

Books

Andrews, Robert Hardy, *Corner of Chicago*, (Boston: Little Brown and Company, 1963).

Dethloff, Henry C., *A Bookmark* (College Station: Texas A&M University Press, 1999).

Martínez, Elizabeth Coonrod, *Josefina Niggli, Mexican American Writer* (Albuquerque: University of New Mexico Press, 2007).

Perry, George Sessions. *Texas: A World in Itself* (New York: Whittlesey House / McGraw Hill, 1942).

Peyton, Green, *San Antonio: City in the Sun* (New York: McGraw-Hill Book Company, 1946).

Articles

For newspaper and magazine articles made available to the author from private collections, the publication data may be missing, hence the omission.

Andrews, Robert. "She Knows the Arctic But Stays Home," 8 October 1931.

Clift, Cecil. "Rosengren Donates Rare Books to IWC." *San Antonio Express*, 15 December 1980.

Diehl, Suzanne. "Prop Master Carries Card, Check." *North San Antonio Times*, 16 April 1981, p. 2.

Goetz, Robert. "Terrell Hills' Frank Duane Writes for Stage and TV." *North San Antonio Times*, 13 February 1986, p. 11.

Gualano, Michele. "Rosengren Wrote and Produced for Stage and TV." *San Antonio Express-News*, 29 April 2010.

Igo, John. "Florence Kednay Rosengren." *North San Antonio Times*, 25 August 1988, p. 5.

Jarboe, Jan. "Bookstore Boot Shabby Shame." *San Antonio Express-News*, April 1982.

Lindee, Susan. "A Couple of Bookworms." *San Antonio Light*, 30 September 1984, I-3.

Lippman, Laura. "It's Too Late for the Literature Starved Fans of Rosengren's." *San Antonio Light*, 26 July 1987.

Lowman, Al. "Changing Times: The Life and Death of a Bookstore." *Southwestern Historical Quarterly*, No. 2, October 1987, pp. 173-184. Republished in *AB Bookman's Weekly*, 14 March 1988, pp. 1069-1074.

McGaffey, Edna. "Booking a Success Story." *San Antonio Express-News*, 26 February, 1978.

Miga, George. "Explorer Donates Books to Library." *Hammond Times*, 17 October 1965, p. 17.

Milligan, Bryce. "Chief Guardian of Civilization." *San Antonio Monthly*. April 1987.

_____. "Bidding Farewell to a Texas Institution." *San Antonio Light*, 26 July 1987, J-16.

_____. "Rosengren Was The Ultimate Bookwoman." *San Antonio Light*, 28 August 1988, K-13.

_____. "Rosengren's Books: An Island of Culture." *Vortex: A Critical Review*, 1988.

Phelon, Craig. "The Author's Best Friend." *San Antonio Express-News*. 19 December 1982, Sunday Magazine, p. 8.

_____. "The Rosengren Family." *San Antonio Express-News*, 3 August 1986, Sunday Magazine, pp. 4-9.

Rosengren, Frank. "My Education as a Bookseller." 1948, 1-21. Unpublished typescript.

Wieters, Denise Herrera. "Doors to Close at Rosengren's." *San*

Antonio Express-News, 17 July 1987.

Young, Gaylon Finklea. "A Giant Among Book-stores." *San Antonio*, September 1975, 27-30.

Interviews and Correspondence

Except where noted, interviews were conducted by the author in San Antonio, Texas. All correspondence listed was in response to inquiries by the author.

Attanasio, Lola Belle Curbo. "Memories of the Rosengrens During World War 11." Letter, dated 25 February 1998, 1-4.

Buchanan, Garland and Sally. Interview conducted 10 July 1996.

Cauthorn, Julia. Interview conducted 18 January 1995.

Cousins, Maggie. Interview conducted 13 February 1995.

Dewar, R.L. Letter, dated 13 February 1999.

Douglas, John. Undated letter.

Ferry, Emily Rosengren. Interview conducted 8 August 1996.

Garrett, Jenkins. Letter, dated 11 March 1997.

Hardberger, Phillip and Linda. Interview conducted 7 February 1995.

Igo, John. Interview conducted 11 January 1995.

Kendall, Dorothy Steinbomer. Interview conducted 15 February 1995.

Kennan, Kent. Interview conducted 3 April 1995.

Lee. Amy Freeman. Interview conducted 28 October 1994.

Leeper, John Palmer. Interview conducted 13 March 1995.

Lowman, Al. Interview conducted in San Marcos, Texas 25 March 1996.

Lowman, Al. Letter, dated 1 October 1997.

Levi, Jocelyn. Interview conducted 14 April 1995.

Maggs, Edward. Interview conducted in London, UK, 20 May 1997.

Maverick, Maury. Letter, dated 22 March 1995.

Moss, Ethel. Interview conducted in Garland, Texas, 7 January 1997.

Rosengren, Frank Duane. Letters, dated 1 April 1995, 26 May 2008, 30 August 2008, 5 November 2008, 30 November 2008 and 28 February 2009.

Rosengren, Frank and Camille. Interviews conducted 2 July 1996, 16 January 1997, and 5 February 1997.

Schorr, Daniel. Interview conducted 4 November 1997.

Taylor, Dr. Gerald. Letter, dated 8 February 1997.

Tobin, Robert Lynn Batts. Interview conducted 30 January 1995.

Index

Photographs and captions shown in italics.

Abbott, John: 46
Abrams, Jacques: 52-54, 61
acequia route, ancient (San Antonio):
    28, 118 notes
A.C. McClurg & Co. bookstore: 4-5
Alamo, the: 28, 69-70, 81-82, 85
Alamo, Battle of: 70, 97
Alamo Plaza: 57, 71, 85, 97, 102 notes
Allen, Fred: 10, 116 notes
Allen, Paula: 92, 121 notes
American Booksellers Association:
    46, 101
Anastacia street compound. *See*
    Rosengren Homestead,
    Zambrano Homestead.
Anglo-Texan Society: 117 notes, 119
    notes
Annunciata and the Shepherds: 51
Antioch College: 29
Apollo, the duck: 52
Apologia Pro Vita Sua (Cardinal
    Newman, London, 1864): 36
Associated American Artists: 65, 69
Ater, Benji: 59
Attanasio, Lola Curbo: 123 notes
Attanasio, Nick: 58
Ayres, Atlee B. and Robert M.: 32, 68
Barclay, Bobby: 38
Bass, Lee: 83
Bass, Nancy Lee: 83
Bass, Perry: 83
Bass, Ramona Seeligson: 83
Beaudoin, Nicki. *See* Prevou, Nicki.
Bedicek, Roy: 76, 126 notes
Bell, Lynn: 89
Bemelmans, Ludwig (books by): 101
Benedict, Burt: 58
Berlin, Irving (song by; sheet music
    of): 5-6
Bernard, Herschel "Herkie": xii
Bexar County Free Library: 44
Bippy, the dog: *98*
Bodenheim, Max: *xvi*

Bolshoi Ballet: 84
Bonham, James: 70
Bonham Street: ii, 64, 70, 79, *81, 82,*
    87, 89-91
bookstores (other than Rosengren's):
—Chicago: A.C. McClurg & Co.,
    4-5; Powner's, 5
—London: Foyles, 32, 119 notes
—San Antonio: general history,
    122-123 notes; Henry A. Moos
    Books, 123 notes; H.R. Higgins
    Books, 88, 127 notes; Nic Tengg's,
    122-123 notes; On Paper, 121
    notes; Sidney P. Gamble's, 123
    notes; Twig Book Shop, 123
    notes, 127-128 notes; Village
    Books, 121 notes; Viva, 123 notes;
    Waldenbooks, San Antonio,
    91-92
Bowen, David: 121 notes
Brackenridge Park: 25, 30, 119 notes
Brando, Marlon (family): 20-21
Braniff, Thomas: 67
Brock, Norman (bookstore): 85
Brooks Field: 46
Brown, Montagu Kingsmill: 75, 82
Browne, Hetty: 25, *27,* 28-29,
    117-118 notes
Browne, Sibyl: 29, 117-118 notes
Buchanan, Bob: 92
Buchanan, Garland: 92-93
Buchanan, Sally: 93
Burnside, Judy: *96*
Butt, Charles "Charlie": 69
Butt, Howard E.: 82
Butt, Mary Elizabeth Holdsworth:
    82
Byrd, Admiral Richard: 11
Cacti of the Southwest, The: 74, 103
    app.
Campbell, Mrs. Patrick: 14
Catholic Theater Guild: 63
Cerf, Bennett: 35, 38

Chatterton, Thomas (book by): 80

Chicago: 3-5, 11

Chicago:

—Humboldt Park: 3-4

—"Chicago Literary Renaissance," 6-7, 115 notes

—wealth of bookstores: 21

Chicago Daily News ("Mid-Week Magazine"): 18, 20, 116 notes

Chiquita, the horse: 30

Christiansen, Gayla (Texas A&M University Press): 103, 125 notes

Cohen, Dave: *94*

Cole, Sylvan: 65

Colosimo, "Big Jim": 6

Columbia University (New York): 28-29

Contine, Brian (University of Texas Press): 103

Cook, Frederick Albert: 11

Corona Press: 95, 121 notes

Cortes, Ernesto "Ernie" (Jr.): xii

Crane, Stephen: 23

Crockett Hotel: 69, *87*, 89, 90

Cry of Peacocks: 58

Cullum, Jim: 118 notes

Curbo, Lola Belle: 57-58

Darnell, Lennie: 59

Davenport, Dora: 51

Davis, Halsey: 54-55, *55*, 61

Dethloff, Henry C: 76

Dewar, Hal: 37

Dewar, Robertson & Pancoast: 34

Dictionary (Dr. Johnson, London, 1755): 36

Dewey, John: 29

Diehl, Suzanne (article by): 128 notes

Dobie, J. Frank: 38, 61, 70, 76, *81* 126 notes, 128 notes

Doty, William (dean, University of Texas): 56

Dos Passos, John (books by): 42

Douglas, John: 47-48, 123 notes

Drayton, Mimi: 58

Drought, Frank: 43

Drury, Dewitt: 59

Drought, Mrs. Henry P. (Sunday salons of): 43

Dugger, Ronnie: *90*, 91, 97, 126 notes

Duke, Cordelia Sloan (book by): 75

Elma Dill Russell Spencer Foundation Series: Texas A&M University Press, 77, 108-110 app.; UT Press, 74-75,77, 103-104

Encino Press: 112 app. *See also* Wittliff, William.

Fehrenbach, T.R.: *90*

Fenstermaker, Rowena: 29

Ferry, Emily Rosengren: *92*

—personal life and career: 72, 100-101

—memories of grandmother, Florence Rosengren: 47, 48, 99-100, 101

Ferry, Steve: 100

Field Museum, Chicago: 11

Fifty Years: 78

First Federal Savings and Loan Association: 69

Fonda, Henry: 63

Ford, O'Neil: 83, 84, 89

Ford, Powell & Carson Architects: 69, 89

Fort Sam Houston: 46, 49, 53, 55, 94, 123-124 notes

Foster, Stephen (sheet music of): 6, 36

Foyles bookshop (London): 32, 119 notes

Francis, Irene: 44

Francklyn Land and Cattle Company: A Panhandle Enterprise 1882-1957: 75, 104 app.

Frantz, Joe Bertram: 75, *81*, 82

Froebel League, New York City: 29

Frost, Eleanor: 38

Frost, Robert: 38-40, *39*, 121 notes

Gattaca (film): 101

Geisel, Theodor Seuss ("Dr. Seuss"): 38

George, Eugene: 116, 119, 120, 124 (all) notes

George Storch Memorial Library (Trinity University): 46

Gilcrease Oil Co.: 34

"Gilcrease" (S.A. bookstore client): 36

Goggan, Hal: 38

Gonzalez, Henry B.: 54

Goodrich, Joe: 59

Gould, Burney: 59

Goyen, William: *81*

Graham, Don (book by): 95

Graham, Martha: 29

Grant, Lyman: *94*

Granz, Norman: 58-59

Graves, John: *81*

Greene, Graham: 23-24, 32, 117 notes

Green, Mary Vance: 29

Green, Rowena. *See* Rowena Fenstermaker.

Grothaus, Julia Ellen: 44, 80

Guaranty Abstract Title Company: 34, 71

Hamilton, Rawlings "Rolly": 62-65, *64, 66,* 69, 71-72, 91, 95

Hamilton, Richard: 65

Hansen, Harry ("The First Reader" column): 18, 117 notes

Hardberger, Amy: 86

Hardberger, Linda: ix, 85

Hardberger, Phillip "Phil": (introduction by) ix-xiii, 85, 127 notes

Harper's Magazine: 70

Harry Ransom Humanities Research Center (University of Texas): 61, 78, 125 notes

Harte, Ed: 82

Harte, Houston (*In Our Image*): 126-127 notes

Harte, Janet: 82

Heard, Daisy: 36

H.E. Butt Foundation: 82

Hecht, Ben: *xvi,* 7

"Herffs," the: 36

HemisFair '68: 73, 84, 100, 113 notes, 114 notes, 121 notes

Hertzberg, Anna Goodman: 119 notes

Hertzberg Circus Collection and Museum: 117 notes, 122 notes

Hertzberg, Harry: 21-22, 23-25, 32, 34, 44, 62, 117 notes, 120 notes, 122 notes

Hill Country State Natural Area: 77

Howes, Wright: *xvi,* 116 notes

Igo, John: 78-80, 126 notes

Incarnate Word High School: 73

Incarnate Word College: 41, 72, 100

independent bookstores, praise of/ demise of: 93-94, 97

Ingram book distributors: 93

Institute of Texan Cultures: 73, 126 notes

"Jacalita", the: 28, 118 notes. *See also* Anastacia street compound.

Jacobs, Bonnie Sue (article by): 118 notes

Japanese Tea Garden: 31

Jarboe, Jan (*SA Express-News* column by): 89-90, 128 notes

J.E. and L.E. Mabee Library (University of the Incarnate Word): 121 notes

Jernigan, Verdayne: 50

Johnston, Leah C.: 44

Jones, Margo: 72, 113 app.

Joske's department store: 71, 97, 122 notes

Kangaroo Court: 93

KBAC radio station: 63

Kednay, Ben: 11

Kednay, Blanche: 11-12, 14, 20, 21, 116 notes

Kednay, Florence. *See* Rosengren, Florence.

Kednay, John Vincent: 11-12, 14, 20

Kednay, Will: 11

Kennan, George: 57

Kennan, Kent: 56-57, 59, 60

Kelly Field: 46, 49

Kent, Jack: 72

Kent, Rockwell: 11-12

Kessel, Dimitri: 59

Keystone School: 73

Kilpatrick, Charles: xiii

Kilpatrick, Margie: xiii

"King Aroo": 72

King James Bible (London, 1611): 36, 120 notes

King of Spain: 25

King Ranch family: 37
KLRN-TV: 73, 114 notes
Knopf, Alfred: 38, 78
Knopf papers (Harry Ransom
    Humanities Research Center),
    UT: 78
Kubik, Gail: 59
La Babia ranch (Musquiz,
    Coahuila): 38
Lackland Training Base: 46
Lady Chatterley's Lover: 41
Lambert's Beach: 30
Lanier, Sydney: 23
"La Piedrera": 31
Laurie, James W.: 46
Lavery, Emmett (play by): *64*
La Villita: 29
Lawrence, D.H. (book by): 41
Lee, Amy Freeman: 51, 60, 68, 82
Leeper, Blanche: 68
"Leeper Colony": 84
Leeper, John Palmer: xii, 67-69, 82,
    125 notes
Lenski, Lois: 71
Letters of Roy Bedichek: *94*
Lewis, Dr. Winford Lee: 12
*Life of Graham Greene: 1904-1939,
    The*: 117 notes
Lilly, J.K. (E. A. Poe collector): 18,
    117 notes
Lilly Library: 117 notes
Lindsey, John H.: 76
Lodovic, Georgette. *See* Georgette
    Sweeney.
Lonesome Dove: 95
Lord, Walter: *81*
Loughridge, Walter: 34, 62, 124
    notes
Louise Lindsey Merrick Natural
    Environment Series (Texas A&M
    University Press): 77, 106-108
    app.
Lowman, Al: 37, 95, 125-126 notes,
    128 notes
Lowrey, Janette Sebring: 43, 51, 78,
    126 notes
MacArthur, Charles: *xvi*
Madeline books: 101

Maggs Bro. Ltd. (London): 36, 55,
    120-121 notes
Maggs, Frank: 36, 120 notes
Man That Was Used Up, The (by E. A.
    Poe), first edition: 15
Magurn, Blanche. *See* Leeper,
    Blanche.
Magurn, Ruth: 68
Main Plaza (San Antonio): 85, 86,
    124 notes, 127 notes
Matilda (film): 101
Maverick, Maury Jr.: xii, 83, *90,*
    127 notes
Maverick, Maury Sr.: xii, 36, 127
    notes
Maverick, Samuel: 65
McCombs, Holland: 59
McAllister, Walter Sr. (San Antonio
    mayor): xiii
McMurtry, Larry: *81*, 95-96, *96*
McNay, Marion Koogler: 67-68
McNay (Marion Koogler) Art
    Museum: xii, 67-69, 82, 85, 125
    notes; Tobin Wing, 67, 69
Melcher, Frederick (*Publishers
    Weekly*), 4
Menger Hotel: 71, 82
Merrill Lynch Rauscher Pierce: 34
Merrick Bar-O Ranch: 77
Merrick, Louise Lindsey: 77, 82
Metropolitan Museum of Art: 72
Mexican-Americans, discrimination
    against: 54
Mexican Consulate office (Milam
    Bldg.): 38
Mexico, country of: 23, 29, 38, 40,
    50, 62
Mielziner, Jo: 65
Milam Building: 24, 32, *33*, 34, 37,
    38, 43, 57, 60, 62, 119 notes
Miller, Henry (books by): xii, 42
Milligan, Bryce: 97, 121 notes, 125
    notes, 130 app.
Minerva, the duck: 52
M.K. Brown Range Life Series (UT
    Press): 75, 104-105 app.
Morgan Library (New York): 17-18
Morris, Willie: 70, *81*

Moses Pitt Atlas: 14
Moss, Ethel Marie: 51, *55*, 60, *66*, 95
The Murders in the Rue Morgue (E. A. Poe), first edition: 15, 17-18
Niggli, Josefina: 50
North San Antonio Times: 73, 118 notes, 128 notes
Nuts at the Roundtable, The: 30, 113 notes
O'Casey, Sean (pamphlet by): 87
Ogden, Dale: 46
O. Henry (pen name for William Sydney Porter): 23
"Omnibus" (CBS series): 72, 113 app.
Our Lady of Sorrows Catholic Church: 31, 118-119 notes
Our Lady of the Lake University: 30, 71
Owens, William A.: *94*
Oxford University Press: 45, 127 notes
Painted Walls of Mexico: 74, 103 app.
Patio Club (Menger Hotel): 82
Pearl Brewery redevelopment: 86, 123 app.
Perry, George Sessions (*Texas: A World In Itself*): 24-25, *81*
Plaza Hotel (San Antonio): 23, 32
Poe, Edgar Allan (first editions): 15, 17-18, 117 notes
Poky Little Puppy, The: 51, 126 notes
Politician: The Life and Times of Lyndon Johnson, The: *90*, 91
Porter, Katherine Anne: 38
Powner's Book Store (Chicago): 5
Preston Northrup (Texas Railroad Commission): 34
Prevou, Nicki Beaudoin: 87, 92
Price, Morgan: 118 notes, 123 notes
Principal Properties (Canadian developer): 89
publishers' reps, importance of: 35, 120 notes
Publishers Weekly: 4, 97
Raging Bull: 101
Rainey, Homer P. (UT president): 61
Random House: 35
Randolph Field: 46, 53, 56

Red Carpet (San Antonio club): 86-87, 89
Reiter, Max: 31-32
Right Stuff, The (film): 101
Rivera, Diego: 29
River Road Country Day School, San Antonio: 25, *26*, *27*, 28-30, 51, 72, 86, 111 app., 117-118 notes, 127 notes
River Road neighborhood, San Antonio: 25, 30-32, 86, 118 notes
Roadside Flowers of Texas, The: 74-75, 103 app.
Romberg, Sigmund (sheet music of): 6
Rommel, Dayton. *See* Drayton, Mimi.
Rosengren, Andrew: 3
Rosengren, Camille "Cam" (Sweeney): *ii*, ix, *92*, 95
—bookstore, taking the helm of: daily management and challenges of, 73, 86, 92; relationship with libraries, 94; navigating evictions and moves, 88-92; notable book sale to Robert Tobin, 125 notes
—early life and family ties: as frequent bookstore customer, 71; growing up in SA hotels, 71; library education, Our Lady of the Lake, 71; meeting "Figgi" and marriage to, 62, 71-72, 112 app.; motherhood, 72; move to and from East Coast, 72; parents of, 71
—museum work: for Institute of Texan Cultures (San Antonio), 73; for Metropolitan Museum of Art (New York), 72
—remembrances: oral history of, 118 notes
Rosengren, Carl "Charlie": 3
Rosengren, Cristina: 3-4
Rosengren Collection (DRT Library): 111 app., 117 notes
Rosengren, Emily. *See* Ferry, Emily Rosengren.

Rosengren family history and papers, disposition of: 60-61, 111-112 app., 116-118 notes
—as love story of books: 3

Rosengren, Florence (Kednay) *ii, 13, 19, 90*
—as avid book reader: love of books and breadth of knowledge, x-xi, 48, 61, 70, 99-100; poetry reading group, 42-43; Yeats (W.B.) collection, 54-55
—as bookstore manager ("old-school"):
award from San Antonio Historical Association, 95; book selling as act of love, service: xiii, 41-42, 48, 62, 97, 99-100; commitment to downtown location: 88-89; conduit of friendships among customers, x-xi, 48, 50-59, 74, 78-79, 85; early bookselling experiences (Chicago), 14-15, *19;* eulogy as "ultimate book-woman," 97; eviction challenges, 62-65, 69-70; evolution of store duties: 34, 40, 41-48, 50, 60, 62, 65; feelings about erotica, "sexy" books, xi-xii, 41-42; flexibility of hours, 37, 51; as friend, supporter of customers, 42, 50-59, 78-80, 86; ill health of, 89; influence on children, 47-48, 67; influence of Alfred Knopf, 78; matchmaker: book lovers with books, x-xi, 74, 79-80; maternal figure, x, 37, 99; "old school" reputation, 101; relationship, libraries: 43-46, 68-69, 94; relationship, military bases, 43, 45-46; relationship, museums, 68-69; relationship, publishers, 46, 74-77, 78, 101, 103-109 app., 111 app.; relationship, ranching families 37-38; rep for Associated American Artists, 65; stimulator of thought and wisdom, ix, xiii, 48, 97, 101; support of J. Frank Dobie, 61, 70, *81;* "talk" of retirement, 73; vibrancy,

recognition in late life, 86-87, 95
—life events and characteristics of:
cook and hostess, 42, 50-59; curiosity, intelligence, and sharp memory: x-xi, 28, 40, 100; death, 97; early life, 11-12; effect of Frank Sr.'s ill health and death, 50-52, 59, 62, 99; energy, optimism and spirit of, 11, 42, 48, 62, 70, 99; friendship with WWII draftees: 49-61; influence of Catholic church, 12, 41-42, 48, 97, 119 notes; letter-writer and recipient, 56, 60-61, 70, 110 app.; meeting and marriage to Frank Sr., 11-12; motherhood, 12, 14; as musician and music-lover, 12, 31, 52; parents of, 11-12; talent with hands: piano, typing: 12; social conscience of, 12, 54, 59; university education, 12, *13,* 28; warmth and generosity, xiii, 52, 80, 83, 87, 99-100

Rosengren, Frank Duane ("Figgi"): *ii, 19,* 112-113 app.
—career of, as writer and producer:
columnist for *San Antonio Light, North San Antonio Times,* 73; executive producer at KLRN-TV, 73, 113-114 app.; first play published, 30, 113 app; list of plays and screenplays by, 113 app; move to East Coast, 72; work in Mexico City (Churusbusco Studios), 62, 71, 113 app.; as writer for "Omnibus" CBS TV series, 72, 112 app.; pen name "Frank Duane," 30; work for HemisFair '68, 73, 113-114 app.; "Pilgrims to the West," 114 app.
—life events and personal traits of:
early education of, 25, *27,* 28-30, 113 app.; early years in Chicago, 12, 14, *19;* eulogized as a "scholar and gentleman," 114 app.; feeding goat as child, *31;* "Figgi" nickname, 14; happy nature, 14;

health concerns, 21; gift to McNay museum, 69; marriage, 62, 71-72; military service, 59, 60, 71, 113 app.; as neighbor of young Marlon Brando, 20; precociousness of, 25; relationship with bookstore, *ii*, ix, 73; study at University of Chicago, 60, 62, 113 app.; summary of life, legacy, 113-114 app.

—remembrances, observations of: demise of independent bookstores, 93-94; discovery of Frank Sr.'s memoir, 4; Frank Sr.'s show-biz appeal, *2*; oral history of, 118 notes; papers given to DRT Library, 117 notes; Rosengren's Books evolution as SA literary center, 40; Rosengren family's welcome to WWII military, 49, 50-51, 54

Rosengren, Frank Sr. (Knut Henning) *2, 8, 9, 19*

—book-selling career, history of: love of books, 4; book purchases in Europe, 36-37; Brando (Marlon) family help, 20; business education, 4; commitment to hand-picked stock, 15; discovery and sale of rare Poe titles, 15, 17-18; dislike of financial career, 4; early work for Chicago bookstores, 4-5; erotica collection, 41-42; evolution of Chicago-based book businesses, xvi, 6-7, *8, 9*, 10, 14-15, *16, 17, 19*, 20, 21; first store, in Chicago apartment, 7; first SA store in Milam Building, 23, 32; free-lance book scout, 5, 6; letter to J. Frank Dobie, 61; memories in "My Education As A Bookseller," 4, 15, 34, 36, 41; passion for first editions, rare books, 7, 10, 15, 17-20, 34, 36, 41; as Random House publisher's rep, 35; writing of bibliography ("The Americana; "A Bookhunter's Guide), 7, 10, 20, 116 notes

—personal life and character traits: belated honeymoon, 20; charm of, 14; death of, 59, 127 notes; early marriages, 116 notes; escape from Texas heat, 35; ill health, 41, 50, 52, 59, 116 notes; marriage to Florence, 12, 14; military stint, 6; name change, "Knut" to "Frank," *2*; parentws and siblings, 3-4; physical description, eyebrows of, 42, 60; move to San Antonio, 21, 24-25; wanderlust, 4-5

—stage/musical career and interests: as banjo-playing baritone, *2*; collector of sheet music, 6, 36, 115 notes; performances at Grand Hotel and Fox Lake Casino, 5-6; singing for Chicago crime boss, 6; stage name, "Frank Rose," *2*

Rosengren, Gerda: 3

Rosengren Homestead (River Road neighborhood). *See also* Zambrano Homestead.

—family, friend, goat: *31*

—home-away-from-home for WWII draftees: 51-59

—gathering spot, as: 35, 42, 50-59, *55*, 59, 123-124 notes

—location, description: 27, 28, 30-31, 42, 57, 60

—other residents: 72, 118 notes

—pets with personalities, home for: *31*, 52

Rosengren, Kitty: 3, 35

Rosengren's Books (under varied names): *See also* specific family members.

—atmosphere and influence of, beyond a business: as center of culture, discourse, enlightenment, ix-xiii, 37-40, 67, 82, 85, 120 notes; on children's lives, 47-48, 67, 93; as epicenter for SA conservation battles, 63; flexibility of hours, 37, 50-51; as "home" with comfortable chairs, xi, xii, xiii, 85;

Rosengren's Books *continued:*
    as incubator for better citizens, ix,
    xiii; as international magnet for
    famous writers and serious read-
    ers, 38, 40, 49; as oasis for culture-
    starved WWII military, 49, xx; as
    stage for political discourse, xi, 83,
    85; theatrical flair, *64*
—customers and business aspects of:
    art in, 56, 115 notes; book-sign-
    ings (see individual authors);
    business-related papers and other
    documents, 110 app., 116 notes;
    cultured tenants of Milam
    Building, 34; donation of author-
    signed books to UIW, 121 notes;
    evictions, 62, 69; final closing,
    97; importance of publisher's reps,
    35, 120 notes; importance to
    publisher's reps, 46, 101; rare book
    collection, 36, 80, 120 notes; sup-
    plier of British publications, 45;
    sale and display of King James
    Bible (1611), 120 notes; sheet
    music, 36; symbiotic relationship
    with public and institutional
    libraries, 43-46; trade with cus-
    tomers from Mexico, 38, 50;
    trade with military bases, 43,
    45-46; trade with ranching fami-
    lies, 37-38; victim of downtown
    development, 89-91
—locations of, Chicago-area:
    North Michigan Ave., *9, 16,* 17,
    20; North State Street (Tree
    Studio Building), *xvi,* 7, *8,* 17, *19;*
    Sherman Ave. (Evanston), 20-21
—locations of, San Antonio:
    Bonham Street (Crockett Hotel),
    ii, 69-70, *81,* 82, *87,* 89-91; East
    Pecan Street, 63-67, 69; Milam
    Building (Travis and Soledad
    streets), 23, 32, *33,* 34, 37-40, 62,
    64; Losoya, 91-92, 97, 110 notes
—notable characterizations by:
    author Willie Morris, 70; book-
    seller John Douglas, 47-48; for-
    mer SA mayor Phillip

Hardberger, ix-xiii; historian
    Al Lowman, 37; historian Joe B.
    Frantz, 82; newspaper/magazines,
    125 notes, 128 notes; poet Robert
    Frost, 38-40, *39; Texas Monthly,*
    78; writer and artist Amy
    Freeman Lee, 82; writer
    and former state rep. Maury
    Maverick Jr., 83; writer Green
    Peyton Wertenbaker, 120 notes
Rudolf Steiner School (New
    York): 72
St. Anthony Hotel: 38, 63, 71
St. Mark's Episcopal Church: 63
St. Martin's Hall (Our Lady of the
    Lake University): 30
St. Michael's Catholic Church: 84
Salek, Joe: 83
Salzmann, Katharine A. (Wittliff
    Collections, Texas State U.): 112
    app.
San Antonio, city of:
—appeal and descriptions of: 21-22,
    23-25, 32, 49
—deficits of: 35, 49, 84, 88
—"makers of": 29
—250th anniversary, HemisFair '68:
    73, 84, 100, 113 notes, 114 notes,
    121 notes
—welcome to Rosengren family:
    24-25
San Antonio: City in the Sun (book):
    120 notes
San Antonio Conservation Society:
    43, 65, 93, 124 notes
San Antonio Express-News: xiii, *89,*
    114 app.
San Antonio Historical Association
    (award by): 95
San Antonio Light: 73, 97
San Antonio Little Theater: 63, 83
San Antonio Museum of Art: 86
San Antonio Public Library: 43-44,
    80, 115 notes
San Antonio River 25, 28
San Antonio River Walk: 86
San Antonio Symphony Orchestra: *64*
Sandburg, Carl: *xvi*

San Fernando Cathedral (San Antonio): 23
San Francisco: 24
Sawyer, Inez: 29
Schorr, Daniel: 52-54, 58, 61, 123-124 notes
Schuette, Dale: 89
Sea Shells of the Texas Coast: 74, 103 app.
Seeligson, Arthur: 83
Seeligson, Frates: x, 83, *90*
Seeligson, Linda Nixon: 83
Sheffy, Lester Fields (book by): 75, 104 app.
Sherry, Norman: 117 notes
Shields, Sue: 47, 65, 86, 92, 95
Sibley, Bill (oral history by): 118 notes
Sinkin, Fay: 79
Sitwell, Edith: 38
Sitwell, Osbert: 38
Six Thousand Miles of Fence: Life on the XIT Ranch of Texas: 75, 104 app.
Slick-Urschel Oil Co.: 34
Smith-Young Tower: 32, 119 notes
Southwestern Writers Collection: *See* Wittliff Collections.
Spencer, Elma Dill: 74-75, 77
Steelesmith, Robert: 86
Steinbomer, Dorothy: 42
Steinbomer, Henry: 42
Steinbomer, Shirley: 42
Strickland, William: 58
Sullivan, Jerry: 91
Sunken Garden Theater: 31-32
Symphony Society of San Antonio: 32
Swartz, Jeff: 92
Sweden: 3, 35
Sweeney, Camille. *See* Rosengren, Camille.
Sweeney, Emmett: 34, 71, 83
Sweeney, Georgette Lodovic: 71
Taylor, Dr. Gerald. 55-56, 60
Texas: A Literary Portrait: 95
Texas: A World in Itself. See Perry, George Sessions.
Texas Folklore Society: 61
Texas Institute of Letters: 61

Temple Beth-El Players: 65
Texas A&M University Press: 74, 76-77, 103 app., 105-110 app., 125 notes
Texas Library Association (award by): 82
Texas Memorial Museum: 74
Texas Monthly: 78
Texas Parks and Wildlife Department: 77
Texas Parks & Wildlife Magazine: 76-77, 105-106 app.
Texas State University. *See* Witliff Collections.
Texasville: 95-96, *96*
Texas Wildlife: Photographs from Texas Parks & Wildlife Magazine: 77, 105 app.
Theodore Gentilz: Artists of the Old Southwest: 74-75, 104 app.
Thomas Jefferson High School: 30, 59
Tick, the cat: 52
Tinkle, Lon: *81*
Tobin Aerial Survey: 67
Tobin Center for the Performing Arts: xii
Tobin Collection of Theatre Arts: 85. *See also* McNay Art Museum.
Tobin, Edgar: 67
Tobin, Margaret Batts: 69
Tock, the dog: 52
Tobin, Robert Lynn Batts: xii, 67-69, 82, 84, 87, 124-125 notes
Travis Park: 32, 63, *64*, 65, 67, 69, 92
Tree Studio Building and Annexes (Chicago): *xvi*, 7, 11, 88, 115–116 notes
Trinity University: 46, 79, 94
Tuggle, Emmit: xiii
Tuggle, Mae: xiii
University of Chicago: 11-12, 60, 62, 88
University of the Incarnate Word. *See* Incarnate Word College.
University of South Carolina Press: 74
University of Texas Press: 74-76, 77, *94*, 103-105 app., 126 notes

Upjohn, Richard: 63
Ustinov, Peter: 100
Van Norturick, Jacque: *87*
Veltman, Hap: 91
Verdi, Guiseppe (opera by): 84
Viva Max (film): 100
Waldenbooks: 91-92
Wallenborn, Robert: 58, 61
Walls Rise Up (by Frank Duane
    Rosengren): 72, 113 notes
Wardlaw, Frank: 74-77, 103, 125
    notes
WAVES (U.S. Naval Reserve,
    Alamo Plaza): 57-58
Webb, Walter Prescott: 76, 126 notes
Weinstock, Herbert (Knopf): 78
Wells, Juanima: 44
Wertenbaker, Green Peyton: 120
    notes
Wilde, Oscar: 23
Williams, Tennessee (book by): 80
Willis, George: 32
Wills, Mary Motz (paintings of):
    74, 103 app.
Wittliff Collections (Southwestern
    Writers Collection, Alkek Library,
    Texas State University): 111 app.,
    116 notes, 128 notes
Wittliff, William: 111-112 app.
Wright, Grace: 79
Witte Museum: 30
Wolfson, Kenneth: 118 notes
Wonner, Paul: 58, 60
World War I: 6, 7, 12, 49
World War II: 36, 49-59, 119 notes,
    123 notes
Yale University: 72
Yeats, William Butler: 23, 54-55
Zambrano Homestead: 24-25, *26,
    27*, 28-31, 118 notes. *See
    also* Rosengren Homestead.
Zambrano, Macario: 25
Zisman, Sam: 83

Colophon

This first edition of *Rosengren's Books: An Oasis for Mind and Spirit*, by Mary Carolyn Hollers George, has been printed on 70 pound Fortune Matte coated paper, containing a percentage of recycled fiber. Titles have been set in Parisian and Colonna type, the text in Adobe Caslon type. All Wings Press books are designed and produced by Bryce Milligan.

Fifty-two copies have been bound in leather. These copies are numbered and signed by the author, the publisher, and Camille Rosengren.

On-line catalogue and ordering:
www.wingspress.com

Wings Press titles are distributed
to the trade by the
Independent Publishers Group
www.ipgbook.com
and in Europe by
www.gazellebookservices.co.uk

Also available as an ebook.